D0448674

Learning by Teaching

Selected Articles on Writing and Teaching

Learning by Teaching

Selected Articles on Writing and Teaching

Donald M. Murray

BOYNTON/COOK PUBLISHERS, INC.

Copyright © 1982 by Donald M. Murray. All rights reserved. No part of this book may be used or reproduced in any manner without written permission except in the case of brief quotations embodied in critical articles and reviews.

For information address Boynton/Cook Publishers, Inc.
206 Claremont Avenue, Montclair, NJ 07042

ISBN: 0-86709-025-1

Printed in the United States of America

83 84 85 10 9 8 7 6 5 4 3 2

Preface

I have apprenticed myself to two trades I can never learn: writing and teaching. These articles are not a record of what I have learned as much as they are a record of what I was learning through their writing. I discover what I'm beginning to know as it appears on the page.

I hope these articles are more questions than answers, that they will stimulate readers to make use of their own experiences at the writing desk and in the classroom workshop to discover what is meaningful about these crafts of discovery. I also hope that sharing my own thoughts and feelings will bring some companionship to those who are engaged in these lonely trades. We need to share how we write and how we teach if we are to continue to learn.

I have not read over my articles before. I find that almost impossible to do. The reality never equals the dream. Reading my own prose I feel a sense of despair. Issac Bashevis Singer says that the wastebasket is the writer's best friend; but these pieces have been published, for the most part, and it is too late. I find that writing is rewriting, and I've been tempted to rewrite these articles. But that seemed dishonest somehow. The ones that have been published are reprinted as they were published. Any examples of sexist language in the early articles are an embarrassing reminder of how long it took our profession to become educated. The articles, for good or bad, reflect how I thought and felt and wrote at the time they were written.

The pieces are not in chronological order. They are arranged in a manner that I hope will be helpful to those who read the book. The first half includes articles that concentrate on trying to understand the writing process, the second half on those that emphasize my understanding of the teaching process. I realize, however, that there is a constant interaction, in all my articles, between the issues of writing and those of teaching. I've found that I've learned a great deal about writing by teaching and a great deal about teaching by writing.

I'm grateful to the academic communities, especially the Conference on College Composition and Communication and the National Council of Teachers of English, its parent body, that have given me the chance to talk and to publish, to listen and to read, to be part of an exciting profession in a period of significant growth. I have been stimulated and supported by the colleagueship of writing teachers from every part of the English-speaking world.

I also appreciate the contributions of my closest colleagues, whose help I see on every page. Those who deserve special appreciation are Thomas Carnicelli, Lester Fisher, Donald Graves, Thomas Newkirk, and Susan Sowers. Most of all, I appreciate the support of my wife, Minnie Mae, to whom all of these pieces have been dictated, not once, but many times. She is the one who has seen the despair caused by all the false drafts, and if it were not for her support, that's all there would be, just early drafts of articles I would some day hope to write.

Contents

The Process of Writing

These first four pieces, published over a period of eleven years, are efforts to understand the writing process. More than that, I suppose, they express a faith that there is a process, that writing is not magic—or is rarely magic—but the result of a series of logical, cognitive, and affective activities that can be understood, and, therefore, learned.

When this concept first became popular, some people understood the process to be linear and even taught it as a production-line operation. Nancy Sommers, Sondra Perl, and others before them, have pointed out that the process is not linear, but that a writer moves back and forth through the process, which is what I meant all along.

1
The Explorers of Inner Space

Why do writers write? To inform, to persuade, to entertain, to explain, but most of all to discover what they have to say.

The layman believes—and often writes badly himself because of it—that the writer has a complete thought or vision he merely copies down, acting as a stenographer for the muse. A few writers on rare occasions have reported such an experience—but only after years of thinking, reading, and craftsmanlike writing. For most writers the act of putting words on paper is not the recording of a discovery but the very act of exploration itself.

John Updike says, "Writing and rewriting are a constant search for what one is saying." Robert Frost speaks of "...the surprise of remembering something I didn't know I knew." "It begins with a character, usually, and once he stands up on his feet and begins to move," according to William Faulkner, "all I do is trot along behind him with a paper and pencil trying to keep up long enough to put down what he says and does."

We read these writers and see their words rigid, right, frozen on the page, but they found their own writing always moving, ever changing. "Writing to me is a voyage, an odyssey, a discovery, because I'm never certain of precisely what I will find," says Gabriel Fielding. Robert Bolt declares,

Published in *English Journal,* September, 1969.

"Writing a play is thinking, not thinking about thinking. . . ." E.M. Forster adds, "How do I know what I think until I see what I say?" And Alberto Moravia testifies that, "One writes a novel in order to know why one writes it."

There is a mystery in this process, for as Nancy Hale says, "Many an author will speak of writing, in his best work, more than he actually knows." C. Day-Lewis concludes, "I do not sit down at my desk to put into verse something that is already clear in my mind. If it were clear in my mind, I should have no incentive or need to write about it, for I am an explorer. . . . We do not write in order to be understood, we write in order to understand."

For the writer, writing is a process, a way of seeing, of hearing what he has to say to himself, a means of discovering meaning. Most writers are compulsive about their methods of work—the writing hours, the special lapboard, the texture of the paper, the blackness of the ink, the grip of the pen. I believe this is, in part, because they feel a primitive awe before their tools. Something happens as the pen point scratches against the paper that they cannot quite explain. Words, scenes, ideas, phrases, characters, concepts, appear unbidden when the writing is going well, and the writer, surprised, must rationalize these accidents, accept them or reject them, control them and use them.

There are moments of inspiration even in quite ordinary writing. The first two sentences of this article came to me weeks after I was invited by a student of mine, English teacher Carol Hovland to write for Concord *Dial,* the student literary magazine at Concord-Carlisle, Massachusetts, High School. Subconsciously I had thought about the assignment, turning it over, putting it aside, consciously forgetting and unconsciously remembering.

Guilt itched my conscience and finally, as I was drifting into sleep one night, these lead sentences came to me and I carefully etched them into my memory. When morning came I woke slowly and untypically read a while in bed, reluctantly accepted a telephone call, glanced at the *Today* show with detachment and was curt with my family. I tried to protect myself in a way they cannot completely understand, allowing my subconscious to work, avoiding involvement, waiting for the moment when the line tightens and I must draw in my catch. (All metaphors are dangerous or I would describe the feeling of the growing idea as intellectual indigestion, a strange, rumbling, eruptive discomfort.)

I started to make notes on my clipboard, to play with ideas and words, the symbols of ideas, in order to discover their structure. Then I quickly committed myself to a first draft, letting myself go, dictating as fast as my wife can type on the IBM, angry when she asks about a pronoun reference or a comma—damn commas—because the words are coming fast, and I'm trying to see where they are going. This is no time for syntax. Dictating, writing with a pen, typing—there is little difference for me at this stage of the writing process. I'm trying to keep up with the flow of ideas, with the chain reaction which results from one word striking another word. I let the writing run, trying to discover its dimensions, its limits, its natural form. For more than a week I kept picking the article up, fiddling with it, and putting it aside, until this morning when, in spite of other priorities, I had to dictate it again, from the beginning.

It changed as I wrote it. For example, I put the insert in here which I had planned for the first page but was shut out somehow by the rush of the writing. I still ask myself, should this fit here, or does it need to be said earlier that the writer does, of course, usually start out thinking he knows where he is going? The professional writer spends hours, days, even years prewriting, taking careful aim, getting ready, and he is often a compulsive outliner. But he has learned to accept the mercurial conditions of discovery once he begins to write. On the page he experiences happy accidents: the unexpected word gives the poet insight, the character acts independent of the novelist and reveals the story to the writer, the historical trend becomes clear under the historian's pen.

Naturally the writer is irritated, made impatient, even frightened by these mutinous sentences. He hurls crumpled pages across the room, slashes ink through words, amputates and transplants paragraphs as he tries to capture and control his own words so that he will discover his own ideas.

The process of discovery is hard work. I see best not looking out the window, nor living life, but suffering what one writer called "the inspiration of the writing desk." Freedom and discipline, spontaneity and practice, craft and art—how can we describe this never stable process? The writer's steps are never steps; they do not occur simultaneously or separately; they do not always occur in the same order. The writer, fearing change but accepting it, exists in a creative turbulence, tossed between the opposite tensions of creativity and control. And yet there are some stages of this chaotic evolution which can be identified and understood.

First, the writer has a hint of a subject. The writer knows he can't write what ought to be written, but only what can be written. He has to have a feeling of completeness, a hunch of a direction, or a hint of a conclusion before he begins to write. And so he allows ideas to grow in his subconscious, nurturing them, feeding them, examining them, but not harvesting them until they are ripe.

The writer usually has an audience in mind. It may be a well-calculated audience, for he may recognize he has something to say which other people need or want to know, but his sense of audience may also come from a gut faith that by writing what he is discovering about life he will expose himself to others who will recognize what he feels as truth. The writer has faith in himself, in the exploration of what is him, finding objectivity through subjectivity. As Robert Motherwell has said of art, "The more anonymous a work, the less universal, because in some paradoxical way we understand the universal through the personal."

Trying to capture abstractions, the writer hungers for the concrete. He continually seeks the specific revealing act, quotation, statistic which will enable him to nail down and therefore communicate an idea or feeling. The helicopter pilot in Vietnam jams Vicks in his nostrils to shut out the smell of death, and the writer hoards specifics which spark in his readers the "shock of recognition" and complete the arc of communication.

Knowing that form is meaning, the writer seeks a design for his writing, Ernest Hemingway said, "Prose is architecture, not interior decoration." And the writer, obsessed with chaos, has a psychological need to tell himself stories, to find an order in the universe symbolized through the artist's form. The writer's belief in form—the scientific theory, the sonnet, the history, the novel—is testimony of his faith that there can be order in the world, and the form which evolves in the process of writing in itself stands as meaning. Composer Anton Webern stated, "To live is to defend a form." That dark New England poet, Robert Frost, said, "When in doubt there is always form for us to go on with. . . . The background is hugeness and confusion shading away from where we stand into black and utter chaos. . . . To me any form I assert upon it is . . . to be considered for how much more it is than nothing." He also called the poem "a momentary stay against confusion." The writer, first, is a seeker of forms.

The writer, however, not only has to find a subject, an audience, specifics, a form, he has to commit himself to the blank page. He writes to discover, with surprise, disappointment and pride, what he has written. How little he knows of what he thought he knew; how much he knows that he didn't know he knew.

He begins to discover what he has said and, therefore, what he has to say by subjecting himself to his own critical eye, and perhaps the eyes of others who are not blinded by maternity. Now deeply involved in the process of writing he redefines his subject, seeks better specifics, perfects his form—researching, restructuring, rethinking, rewriting—seeking through these perpetual reconsiderations his own meaning.

At last he edits, engaged in a personal struggle with language. Mark Twain reportedly said that "The difference between the right word and the wrong word is the difference between lightning and a lightning bug." Hemingway admitted, "I rewrote the ending to *Farewell to Arms,* the last page of it, thirty-nine times before I was satisfied." The *Paris Review* interviewer asked, "Was there some technical problem there? What was it that had you stumped?" And Hemingway answered, "Getting the words right." The writer is a cold executive, making a thousand decisions in a paragraph, hiring one word, firing another. He is a craftsman who hones a phrase, reads a sentence aloud, moves a word, fits in an idea, shapes a paragraph, scene or chapter. I have polished, shaped, cut down, and built up this article during a dozen readings and rereadings. I don't always enjoy this process for I am lazy, but it is necessary. It comes with the territory. The writer knows he has to make the stubborn personal effort by sweat to discover his meaning so that he will find out precisely what he has said.

There are rewards and excitement, however, for when we discover what we have said we discover who we are. In finding your voice you discover your identity. Style is not a fashionable garment you put on; style is what you are; what you have to say as well as how you say it. We admire people who are natural, who are themselves, and the best way to know yourself and your own world may be to try and write it down.

Your world is the universe you can describe by using your own eyes, listening to your own voice—finding your own style. We write to explore the constellations and galaxies which lie unseen within us waiting to be mapped with our own words.

Now, as I come to the end of this article, still another private experiment with the process of writing, I begin to see, like a photograph slowly evolving in the developer—shadow turning into line—what I have to say because I have dared to try to say it. I have learned about the process of discovery in writing, by writing. But once said, the job is never done, for writing is never final. The writer goes on writing to discover, explore, and map the evolution of his personal worlds of inner space.

2

The Interior View

One Writer's Philosophy of Composition

The process by which the publishing writer discovers what he has to say and says it has important implications for the student writer.

Yet in the English Department composition course we usually limit ourselves to an exterior view of writing, principally examining what has been written or studying patterns which have been evolved by the analysis of what has been published.

The critic, the scholar, the scientist of language and form, all make contributions to the understanding of writing. We all learn, writers certainly included, from what perceptive readers see in a piece of writing, and we can gain new insights into old problems from such stimulating work as that reported by Dr. Robert Zoellner in his article, "A Behavioral Approach to Writing," which made up the entire January 1969 issue of *College English*. More scholars, using information from the social sciences and the sciences, should be encouraged to contribute to the study of the writing process.

There should be, however, serious consideration of the interior view of composing seen by the practicing writer. Since I am declaring my own philosophy of composition, I have to admit my own subjectivity, my own involvement in the process I am to philosophize about. I have been and I am a

Published in *College Composition and Communication*, February, 1970.

writer of fiction and non-fiction. I do not see writing from the exterior view but from within my own mind and my own emotions as I try to write every single day of my life.

My personal exploration of the writing process is supported by an almost lifelong study of the testimony of other writers. I can remember going to the Wollaston Public Library and reading what writers had to say about writing before I was in the Seventh Grade. I have certainly read, and unfortunately purchased, most of the bad books about how to write by writers published in the last quarter century. I've also found some significant ones, and what I have read in those books has been reinforced by the testimony of writers I have known.

But my view of composing is frankly personal. The interior view of the writing act reveals that writing is an individual search for meaning in life. As I have written about the process of writing my main resource has been myself.

For months, even before I wrote this paper, I had been trying to capture the essential process of writing in one sentence. I had been writing, rewriting and revising draft sentences to find out what writing looks like when it is not seen from the outside as an act completed, but when it is seen from the inside as a continuing process. Here is my one sentence:

> A writer is an individual who uses language to discover meaning in experience and communicate it.

Let's see if we can wriggle into the skin of the writer and explore the meaning of this sentence from that point of view. If this sentence stands up it contains some significant—and very specific—implications for the way we teach composition.

A WRITER IS AN INDIVIDUAL
who uses language
to discover meaning in experience
and communicate it.

At the moment of writing the writer has a fundamental aloneness. Although I have written in the city room, suffered group journalism at Time, worked with a collaborator, I have always found that at the center of the process I am alone with the blank page, struggling to discover what I know so I can know what to say.

The scholar or the historian of writing may know that the writer's belief he can find a new way of saying what he has to say is naive. The academic knows that the problems on the writer's page have all been worked out by other writers. But the writer's illusion of innocence is essential. As Frost said, "No surprise for the writer, no surprise for the reader." If the writer does not feel that through writing he will discover something which is uniquely his, he may soon concentrate on craft rather than content and speak with tricks rather than truth.

The good writer, of course, doesn't write entirely for himself, but he must be self-centered. He accepts criticism if he sees its value. He rejects criticism if it will not help him extricate himself from his immediate writing problem. The writer uses the traditions which work for him, and he rejects the traditions which do not work for him. He seeks praise, and he mistrusts it. He is most hungry for success and most fearful of success.

It has never been easy for the writer to maintain his individuality, and it never will be. Listen to Jane Austen, Andre Gide, e. e. cummings, and Stephen Spender, a fascinating quartet to imagine around your dinner table.

Jane Austen says, "No, I must keep to my own style, and go in my own way; and though I may never succeed. . .I am convinced that I should totally fail in any other."

Gide adds, "Look for your own. Do not do what someone else could do as well as you. Do not say, do not write what someone could say, could write as well as you. Care for nothing in yourself but what you feel exists nowhere else—and out of yourself create. . .the most irreplaceable of beings."

"to be nobody—but—yourself—,'" e.e. cummings agrees; "in a world which is doing its best, night and day, to make you everybody else—means to fight the hardest battle which any human being can fight; and never stop fighting."

Stephen Spender says, "The essential fact about the poet is that he is alone with his experience. He relates the new to the unprecedented, but he does so by instinct and intuition, not by established rule. If a poet works on an image and then attempts to judge the truth of his own lines he does so by asking himself, 'Is this how I really saw or experienced it?' not by asking, 'Is this how some other writer whom I approve of would have described it?' "

A writer is an individual
WHO USES LANGUAGE
to discover meaning in experience
and communicate it.

When you sit at the writer's desk, in the writer's skin, you discover his feeling for language as a living tool. He feels language in his fingers, hears language in his ears, sees language evolving and working on his page. He knows language, no matter how much he delights in this tool, is never an end in itself. It is what the writer uses to lead him to understanding. The painter doesn't paint colors he has seen, he uses color on the canvas to see. The composer uses the notes on the piano to hear. The writer doesn't write down words to photograph what is in his head, he uses words to set an experiment in motion.

Words are put down so he can find out what they reveal when they bump into other words on the page. The writer uses verb and noun, phrase and sentence, paragraph and page, to explore his world. Any usage is appropriate if it is honest and illuminating. The writer toys with language, knowing that out of his most irresponsible word play may come his most responsible writing. His drafts, both in his mind and on the page, are filled with words, tried out and discarded, arranged and rearranged—evidence of language that is always changing, flexible, usable.

A writer is an individual
who uses language
TO DISCOVER MEANING IN EXPERIENCE
and communicate it.

"I write to find out what I'm thinking about," says Edward Albee. "Writing and rewriting are a constant search for what one is saying," adds John Updike. And Robert Creeley agrees, "For myself writing has always been the way of finding out what I was thinking about."

"The impulse of the pen," cries Jules Renard, "left alone, thought goes as it will. As it follows the pen, it loses its freedom. It wants to go one way, the pen another. It is like a blind man led astray by his cane, and what I came to write is no longer what I wish to write."

William Carlos Williams sums it all up: "The poet thinks with his poem."

When the reader looks at the published piece of writing he sees something which is absolute, and he may feel that what he sees is a piece of thinking which was completed and then copied down by the writer. When the writer looks at a piece of writing he sees the final chart of a voyage of discovery, and he can imagine the expedition which began with a dream, developed through a series of choices, calculations, failures, successes, accidents and is at last completed.

The writer's basic job is not to say what he already knows but to explore his own experience for his own meaning. His experience may be in the library or in the pub, but at the moment of writing he uses the tool of language to discover the meanings which exist in his experience. As he uses his language to try to put down on the page what he thinks he means he keeps changing the words—he thinks. As his writing develops under his hand his words reveal his meaning, an order evolves as his mind uses language to expose what is significant in his experience.

A writer is an individual
who uses language
to discover meaning in experience
AND COMMUNICATE IT.

During the process of writing the writer has, in a sense, been communicating with himself. And if the words on the writer's page reveal the writer's meaning to himself through language, the writer then can reveal what he has discovered to others and practice Orwell's definition of an effective style, "Good writing is like a windowpane."

The writer should get out of the way of what he has said and let the reader see what is left standing where the writer has worked. He doesn't want the reader to pass through the writer's own experience of discovery.

To communicate effectively the writer may do some final tinkering and make some adjustments in his words, using specialized analogies, for example, to reach a particular audience. But even in the final editing the professional writer doesn't look to the language, but through it to what he has to say, not asking, "Is this the attractive word?" as much as, "Is this the accurate word?" The writer doesn't make adjustments in what he has to say; he doesn't look to the audience first and write down what the reader wants to hear. The good writer communicates by building—through language—a sturdy discovery of thought.

Now we can look back at the complete sentence to see if it expresses the interior view of the process of composing, a constantly changing, evolving, searching act. If we agree this is what the writer goes through then we may be able to say as clearly and succinctly what the student writer should go through.

> A student writer is an individual who is learning to use language to discover meaning in experience and communicate it.

Too often the very word *student* gets in our way, and we forget that the student is simply, first of all, a writer. If he is to write well he has to go through a process similar to the one which the professional writer has found works for him.

I can hear the English teachers ask, "What do a poet's writing processes have to do with my students who can't write a literate term paper?" My answer is: everything. The college freshman may learn something about literature and what another man found in life by reading the poem, and he may learn something about writing by discovering how the poem was made. He will probably learn more, however, looking into his own life and writing his own poem.

The interior view of the writing process makes it clear that the writing course should have one central purpose: to allow the student to use language to explore his world. But if the student does learn to write as the published author writes, he will also be able to do a much better job on the term paper. Practical academic skill and, perhaps, commercial skill are the by-products of a workshop which allows the student to experience the process of writing. We tend to forget the hard cash value the world places on art, not even realizing it is doing it. I have been a ghostwriter because I have been a novelist. Industry, government, the university—the holy trinity of our society—continually tries to hire communicators who can discover order through language and, therefore, reveal it.

We may not be able to teach our students to write, but as teachers we can create an environment which will encourage them to pass through the stages of writing necessary for effective written communication.

A STUDENT WRITER IS AN INDIVIDUAL
who is learning to use language
to discover meaning in experience
and communicate it.

There is no one way to write and there is no one way for the student to learn to write. We must accept the individual student and appreciate his individualness. No class can move lock step through a writing sequence which is meaningful. The students do not start at the same place and they do not end at the same place. They do not proceed at a similar pace and they do not follow the same path through the course. A student writer may rewrite on the page or in his head; he may write slowly or swiftly; he may overwrite or underwrite. What is even more confusing, the same student writer, just like the publishing writer, may do all of these things at different times on different writing projects.

It is true that we, veteran teachers, numbed by years of conferences, will see certain patterns of development repeated in our students. These patterns interest us as teachers, but they are not significant to our students. What John Milton did centuries ago or Jimmy Jones did last semester is of surprisingly little immediate help to the student who has to find his own way. The student should know there is a basic process of writing, practiced by most writers, but ultimately he has to learn the process for himself.

The teacher may comfort and encourage the student with the information that other lonely writers have passed the same way, but the teacher should never make the student feel there is one thing to say, one way to think, one way to speak, one work pattern appropriate for every task. The learning writer should always feel he is working towards the one best way he can say what he has to say, listening to hear his own voice speaking his own meaning.

A student writer is an individual
WHO IS LEARNING TO USE LANGUAGE
to discover meaning in experience
and communicate it.

There are no absolutes in language. The student must get away from the idea of right and wrong in usage and develop the feeling that there is language which works and language which doesn't work, and most of the time you only know what works by trying to make it work. The student should discover language is fun because it is a sturdy tool for the exploration of experience. It gives the student writer what he hungers for—a way to find meaning and understanding in his own experience. The student writer should find out for himself that language is purposeful, that it yields a valuable product: thought.

And to yield this product language should be used wastefully, even promiscuously, because it is usually necessary to use the wrong word to get to the right word and to pass through the awkward construction on the way to the graceful one. While John Kenneth Galbraith was working on a book he called

Why People Are Poor, he decided that title was undescriptive, and he called his manuscript *The Opulent Society*. It was not the right word and Galbraith knew it, but it was getting there. *Opulent* was the necessary wrong word. It was a long step from *Why People Are Poor* to *The Opulent Society*. It was a short step to his celebrated title, *The Affluent Society*.

The exactly wrong word, the clumsy clause, the misplaced modifier, which are too often ruled mistakes in the English course, may be evidence of language being used to lead the mind to meaning. Therefore they are not mistakes in the conventional sense but merely experiments that didn't work, but which may have beneficial side-products. They are only mistakes when they do not communicate the writer's meaning in the final edited draft.

A student writer is an individual
who is learning to use language
TO DISCOVER MEANING IN EXPERIENCE
and communictae it.

The student writer is searching for what is significant in his experience. That is what the writer does and that is what the student does. To allow this search to occur the teacher must realize that not all his students will have the same experience or find the same meaning in the same experience. What is meaningful for the student may not be meaningful for the teacher. And what the teacher believes is significant may have little significance for the student. Too often the most experimental composition course is absolutely rigid because it attempts to impose a theme on an entire class. Our educational system still thrives because there is no one issue which, thank God, has equal relevance to a class of undergraduates meeting at the same hour each week.

As teachers we should, of course, create environments where the student's conclusions are tested. His opinions must be informed and they must stand up after he gets out from under them. But most of all there must be time in the writing course for the process of discovery to take place. The very act of exploration through language adds to the student's experience. He is engaged in a continual process of revision, refinement, definition, and clarification. His words change and therefore his ideas; his ideas change and therefore his words.

A student writer is an individual
who is learning to use language
to discover meaning in experience
AND COMMUNICATE IT.

The importance of communication cannot be minimized, for publication before the eyes of the instructor and possibly the class completes a stage in the writing process. When the writer is convinced he has found what he has to say and has said it as well as he can, then he shows it to the reader. And then, when he has seen his own words with a stranger's eyes, he usually decides he has to go back and rediscover just what he has to say. The writing course does not have the usual police pressure of quizzes and grades. The student writer faces a greater trial. With the publishing writer, he suffers exposure on the page. He is examined by his peers and by his instructor on what he has said, not what he hoped to say.

Through the inevitable self-revelation of the writing course the student discovers a painful essential lesson: you can't write writing. Content always precedes form. If you don't have a subject you won't have a reader; if you don't know what you mean you can't say it; if language does not clarify your own mind it will not clarify your reader's mind.

The interior view of the writing process as it is seen by the publishing writer may challenge the writing teacher to design an educational environment in which his students can make this sentence come alive:

> A writer is an individual who uses language to discover meaning in experience and communicate it.

3

Teach Writing as a Process Not Product

Most of us are trained as English teachers by studying a product: writing. Our critical skills are honed by examining literature, which is finished writing; language as it has been used by authors. And then, fully trained in the autopsy, we go out and are assigned to teach our students to write, to make language live.

Naturally we try to use our training. It's an investment and so we teach writing as a product, focusing our critical attentions on what our students have done, as if they had passed literature in to us. It isn't literature, of course, and we use our skills, with which we can dissect and sometimes almost destroy Shakespeare or Robert Lowell, to prove it.

Our students knew it wasn't literature when they passed it in, and our attack usually does little more than confirm their lack of self-respect for their work and for themselves; we are as frustrated as our students, for conscientious, doggedly responsible, repetitive autopsying doesn't give birth to live writing. The product doesn't improve, and so, blaming the student—who else?—we pass him along to the next teacher, who is trained, too often, the same way we were. Year after year the student shudders under a barrage of criticism, much of it brilliant, some of it stupid, and all of it irrelevant. No matter how careful our criticisms, they do not help the student since when we teach composition we are not teaching a product, we are teaching a process.

And once you can look at your composition program with the realization you are teaching a process, you may be able to design a curriculum which works. Not overnight, for writing is a demanding, intellectual process; but

Published in *The Leaflet,* New England Association of Teachers of English, Fall, 1972.

sooner than you think, for the process can be put to work to produce a product which may be worth your reading.

What is the process we should teach? It is the process of discovery through language. It is the process of exploration of what we know and what we feel about what we know through language. It is the process of using language to learn about our world, to evaluate what we learn about our world, to communicate what we learn about our world.

Instead of teaching finished writing, we should teach unfinished writing, and glory in its unfinishedness. We work with language in action. We share with our students the continual excitement of choosing one word instead of another, of searching for the one true word.

This is not a question of correct or incorrect, of etiquette or custom. This is a matter of far higher importance. The writer, as he writes, is making ethical decisions. He doesn't test his words by a rule book, but by life. He uses language to reveal the truth to himself so that he can tell it to others. It is an exciting, eventful, evolving process.

This process of discovery through language we call writing can be introduced to your classroom as soon as you have a very simple understanding of that process, and as soon as you accept the full implications of that process, and as soon as you accept the full implications of teaching process, not product.

The writing process itself can be divided into three stages: *prewriting, writing,* and *rewriting.* The amount of time a writer spends in each stage depends on his personality, his work habits, his maturity as a craftsman, and the challenge of what he is trying to say. It is not a rigid lock-step process, but most writers most of the time pass through these three stages.

Prewriting is everything that takes place before the first draft. Prewriting usually takes about 85% of the writer's time. It includes the awareness of his world from which his subject is born. In prewriting, the writer focuses on that subject, spots an audience, chooses a form which may carry his subject to his audience. Prewriting may include research and daydreaming, note-making and outlining, title-writing and lead-writing.

Writing is the act of producing a first draft. It is the fastest part of the process, and the most frightening, for it is a commitment. When you complete a draft you know how much, and how little, you know. And the writing of this first draft—rough, searching, unfinished—may take as little as one percent of the writer's time.

Rewriting is reconsideration of subject, form, and audience. It is researching, rethinking, redesigning, rewriting—and finally, line-by-line editing, the demanding, satisfying process of making each word right. It may take many times the hours required for a first draft, perhaps the remaining fourteen percent of the time the writer spends on the project.

How do you motivate your student to pass through this process, perhaps even pass through it again and again on the same piece of writing?

First by shutting up. When you are talking he isn't writing. And you don't learn a process by talking about it, but by doing it. Next by placing the opportunity for discovery in your student's hands. When you give him an assignment you tell him what to say and how to say it, and thereby cheat your student of the opportunity to learn the process of discovery we call writing.

To be a teacher of a process such as this takes qualities too few of us have, but which most of us can develop. We have to be quiet, to listen, to respond. We are not the initiator or the motivator; we are the reader, the recipient.

We have to be patient and wait, and wait, and wait. The suspense in the beginning of a writing course is agonizing for the teacher, but if we break first, if we do the prewriting for our students they will not learn the largest part of the writing process.

We have to respect the student, not for his product, not for the paper we call literature by giving it a grade, but for the search for truth in which he is engaged. We must listen carefully for those words that may reveal a truth, that may reveal a voice. We must respect our student for his potential truth and for his potential voice. We are coaches, encouragers, developers, creators of environments in which our students can experience the writing process for themselves.

Let us see what some of the implications of teaching process, not product are for the composition curriculum.

Implication No. 1. The text of the writing course is the student's own writing. Students examine their own evolving writing and that of their classmates, so that they study writing while it is still a matter of choice, word by word.

Implication No. 2. The student finds his own subject. It is not the job of the teacher to legislate the student's truth. It is the responsibility of the student to explore his own world with his own language, to discover his own meaning. The teacher supports but does not direct this expedition to the student's own truth.

Implication No. 3. The student uess his own language. Too often, as writer and teacher Thomas Williams points out, we teach English to our students as if it were a foreign language. Actually, most of our students have learned a great deal of language before they come to us, and they are quite willing to exploit that language if they are allowed to embark on a serious search for their own truth.

Implication No. 4. The student should have the opportunity to write all the drafts necessary for him to discover what he has to say on this particular subject. Each new draft, of course, is counted as equal to a new paper. You are not teaching a product, you are teaching a process.

Implication No. 5. The student is encouraged to attempt any form of writing which may help him discover and communicate what he has to say. The process which produces "creative" and "functional" writing is the same. You are not teaching products such as business letters and poetry, narrative and exposition. You are teaching a process your students can use—now and in the future—to produce whatever product his subject and his audience demand.

Implication No. 6. Mechanics come last. It is important to the writer, once he has discovered what he has to say, that nothing get between him and the reader. He must break only those traditions of written communication which would obscure his meaning.

Implication No. 7. There must be time for the writing process to take place and time for it to end. The writer must work within the stimulating tension of unpressured time to think and dream and stare out windows, and pressured time—the deadline—to which the writer must deliver.

Implication No. 8. Papers are examined to see what other choices the writer might make. The primary responsibility for seeing the choices is the student. He is learning a process. His papers are always unfinished, evolving, until the end of the marking period. A grade finishes a paper, the way publication usually does. The student writer is not graded on drafts any more than a concert pianist is judged on his practice sessions rather than on his performance. The student writer is graded on what he has produced at the end of the writing process.

Implication No. 9. The students are individuals who must explore the writing process in their own way, some fast, some slow, whatever it takes for them, within the limits of the course deadlines, to find their own way to their own truth.

Implication No. 10. There are no rules, no absolutes, just alternatives. What works one time may not another. All writing is experimental.

None of these implications require a special schedule, exotic training, extensive new materials or gadgetry, new classrooms, or an increase in federal, state, or local funds. They do not even require a reduced teaching load. What they do require is a teacher who will respect and respond to his students, not for what they have done, but for what they may do; not for what they have produced, but for what they may produce, if they are given an opportunity to see writing as a process, not a product.

4

Writing as Process

How Writing Finds Its Own Meaning

At the beginning of the composing process there is only blank paper. At the end of the composing process there is a piece of writing which has detached itself from the writer and found its own meaning, a meaning the writer probably did not intend.

Published in *Eight Approaches to Teaching Composition,* edited by Timothy R. Donovan and Ben W. McClelland, National Council of Teachers of English, 1980.

This process of evolving meaning—a constant revolt against intent—motivates writers. They never cease to be fascinated by what appears on their page. Writing is an act of recording or communicating and much more. Writing is a significant kind of thinking in which the symbols of language assume a purpose of their own and instruct the writer during the composing process.

This process has been revered—and feared—as a kind of magic, a process of invoking the muse, of hearing voices, of inherited talent. Many writers still think that the writing process should not be examined closely or even understood in case the magic disappear. Others of us, instructed by Janet Emig (1975), attempt to understand the relationship between the chemical and electrical interaction within the brain and the writing process. I am sympathetic to both positions, but, as a writer still trying to learn my craft at fifty-four and as a writing teacher still trying to learn how to help students learn their craft, I feel an obligation to speculate upon the writing process.

The process of making meaning with written language can not be understood by looking backward from a finished page. Process can not be inferred from product any more than a pig can be inferred from a sausage. It is possible, however, for us to follow the process forward from blank page to final draft and learn something of what happens. We can study writing as it evolves in our own minds and on our own pages and as it finds its own meaning through the hands of our writer colleagues and our writing students. We can also interview our colleagues, our students, and ourselves about what is happening when writing is happening. We can examine the testimony of writers in published interviews, such as the series of books, *Writers at Work: The Paris Review Interviews,* or in journals, letters, autobiographies, biographies, and manuscript studies. We can also consider the testimony of composers, artists, and scientists. If we attend to such available testimony, we may be able to speculate, with some authority, on how writing finds its own meaning.

But a key problem in discussing—or teaching—the writing process is that in order to analyze the process, we must give unnatural priority to one element of an explosion of elements in simultaneous action and reaction. Meaning is made through a series of almost instantaneous interactions. To study those interactions within ourselves, other writers, or our students, we must stop time (and therefore the process) and examine single elements of the writing process in unnatural isolation.

The danger is that we never recombine the elements. Some teachers present each part of the writing process to their students in a prescriptive, sequential order, creating a new kind of terrifying rhetoric which "teaches" well but "learns" poorly. It will be important for both of us—the reader and the writer—to remember throughout this chapter that we are talking about a process of interaction, not a series of logical steps. As Janet Emig has pointed out to me, we need to apply technology to our writings on process—for example, printing plastic overlays, as some textbooks do to reveal the organs of the body, as a way of showing the simultaneous interaction of the elements of writing process.

If we stand back to look at the writing process, we see the writer following the writing through the three stages of rehearsing, drafting, and revising as the piece of work—essay, story, article, poem, research paper, play, letter, scientific report, business memorandum, novel, television script—moves toward its own meaning. These stages blend and overlap, but they are also distinct. Significant things happen within them. They require certain attitudes and skills on the writer's and the writing teacher's part.

The Stages of the Writing Process

The term *rehearsing,* first used by my colleague Donald Graves (1978) after observation of children writing, is far more accurate than *prewriting* to describe the activities which precede a completed draft. During this stage of the writing process the writer in the mind and on the page prepares himself or herself for writing before knowing for sure that there will be writing. There is a special awareness, a taking in of the writer's raw material of information, before it is clear how it will be used. When it seems there will be writing, this absorption continues, but now there is time for experiments in meaning and form, for trying out voices, for beginning the process of play which is vital to making effective meaning. The writer welcomes unexpected relationships between pieces of information from voices never before heard in the writer's head.

Drafting is the most accurate term for the central stage of the writing process, since it implies the tentative nature of our written experiments in meaning. The writer drafts a piece of writing to find out what it may have to say. The "it" is important. The writing process is a process of writing finding its own meaning. While the piece of writing is being drafted, that writing physically removes itself from the writer. Thus, it can be examined as something which may eventually stand on its own before a reader. This distancing is significant, for each draft must be an exercise in independence as well as discovery.

The final state in the writing process is *revising*. The writing stands apart from the writer, and the writer interacts with it, first to find out what the writing has to say, and then to help the writing say it clearly and gracefully. The writer moves from a broad survey of the text to line-by-line editing, all the time developing, cutting, and reordering. During this part of the process the writer must try not to force the writing to say what the writer hoped the text would say, but instead try to help the writing say what it intends to say.

One of the most important things I have learned, for example, as this piece of writing has detached itself from my intentions and instructed me, is that revision which does not end in publication becomes the most significant kind of rehearsal for the next draft. I had experienced this in my writing and observed it in my colleagues and my students. Yet I did not understand it until I found myself articulating it on these pages. I had never before seen how revising becomes rehearsal as the writer listens to the piece of writing. It may be worth noting that if you drop the "s" in the word rehearsing, it becomes rehearing. The writer *listens* to see what is on the page, scans, moves in closely, uncaps the pen, slashes sections out, moves others around, adds new ones. Somewhere along the line the writer finds that instead of looking back to the previous draft, trying to clarify what has been written, the writer is actually looking ahead to the next draft to see what must be added or cut or reordered. Revising has become rehearsing.

This process of discovering meaning—rehearsing, drafting, revising, rehearsing, drafting, revising, rehearsing—repeated again and again is the way the writing's meaning is found and made clear. This process may be seen in Figure 1.

I had always thought of this process in rather large terms—a period of rehearsing (perhaps minutes, but more likely hours, days, weeks, months), a period of drafting (much shorter but, in the case of a book, measured in months or years), and a period of revising (which is at least as long as rehearsing). But the significant work of Sondra Perl, Director of the Writing Development Project at Lehman College, City University of New York, has made me reconsider the time in which this process works. She writes in the *New York University Education Quarterly* (1979, p. 18):

> Composing does not occur in a straightforward, linear fashion. The process is one of accumulating discrete words or phrases down on the paper and then working from these bits to reflect upon, structure, and then further develop what one means to say. It can be thought of as a kind of "retrospective structuring"; movement forward occurs only after one has reached back, which in turn occurs only after one has some sense of where one wants to go. Both aspects, the reaching back and the sensing forward, have a clarifying effect. . . . Rereading or backward

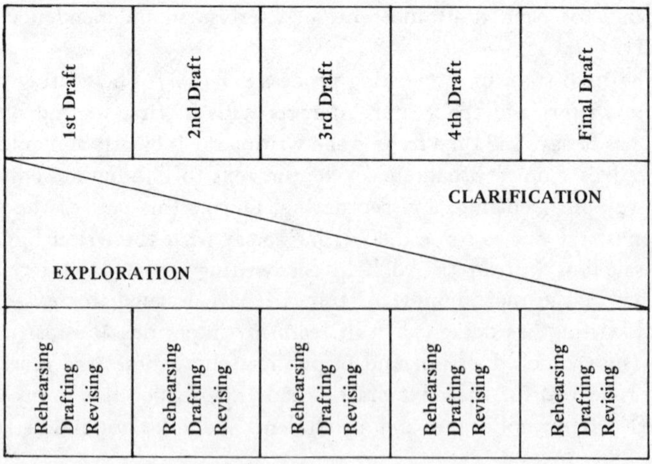

movements become a way of assessing whether or not the words on the page adequately capture the original sense intended. But constructing simultaneously involves discovery. Writers know more fully what they mean only after having written it. In this way the explicit written form serves as a window on the implicit sense with which one began.

Perl's work enabled me to see an instantaneous moving back and forth during the writing process. Minute by minute, perhaps second by second—or less at certain stages of the process—the writer may be rehearsing, drafting, and revising, looking back and looking forward, and acting upon what is seen and heard during the backward sensing and forward sensing.

The writer is constantly learning from the writing what it intends to say. The writer listens for evolving meaning. To learn what to do next, the writer doesn't look primarily outside the piece of writing—to rule books, rhetorical traditions, models, to previous writing experiences, to teachers or editors. To learn what to do next, the writer looks within the piece of writing. The writing itself helps to see the subject. Writing can be a lens: if the writer looks through it, he or she will see what will make the writing more effective.

The closer we move inside the writing process to speculate about how it works, the more we begin to see that what happens in the writer's mind seems much the same thing, whether the writer is rehearsing, drafting, or revising. We can document what happens during the rehearsing and revising process relatively well from the manuscript evidence and writer testimony. We can surmise from a certain authority that what happens during the drafting process is similar; but since it happens so fast, it is often imperceptible. The writer may not even be aware it is happening.

During the processes of rehearsing, drafting, and revising, four primary forces seem to interact as the writing works its way towards its own meaning. These forces are *collecting* and *connecting, writing* and *reading.* Writing may be ignited by any one of these forces in conjunction with any other; but once writing has begun, all of these forces begin to interact with each other. It may be helpful to look at the following diagram to see how these forces interact.

These forces interact so fast that we are often unaware of their interaction or even of their distinct existence. As we collect a piece of information, we immediately try to connect it with other pieces of information; when we write a phrase, we read it to see how it fits with what has gone before and how it may lead to what comes after. To identify these forces at work within the writing process and to understand them, we must artificially halt the interaction and examine one force at a time.

The primary forward motion of the writing process seems to come from man's unlimited hunger for *collecting* information. This need grows from the animal need for food, shelter, and safety to an intellectual need to discover meaning in experience. Man is an information-collecting organism. Information, brought to us through sight, hearing, touch, taste, smell, is stored, considered, and shared. Our education extends the range of our information-collecting through reading and research that reaches back in time and across the barriers of distance and difference.

The volume of material we gather—consciously and sub-consciously—becomes so immense and is so diverse it demands *connecting.* We are compelled to provide some order for the confusion of information or it will drown us. We must discriminate, select the information that is significant, build chains of information which lead to meaning, relate immediate information to previous information, project information into the future, discover from the patterns of information what new information must be sought. The connections we make force us to see information we did not see before. The connections we are making also force us to seek new, supporting information; but, of course, some of that information doesn't support—it contradicts. So we have to make new connections with new information which in turn demands new connections. These powerful, countervailing forces work for and against each other to manufacture new meanings as we live through new experiences.

The writer fears that the collecting apparatus will be excessively controlled by the connecting apparatus. Man's dread of chaos and need for order is so fundamental that writers have to resist the desire for predictable orders, and resist the instinct to fit all new information into previously constructed meanings. The writer has to encourage the gathering of contradictory and unpredictable information which will force old meanings to adapt and new ones to be constructed.

When in good working order, these forces of collecting and connecting battle each other in a productive tension that keeps us intellectually alive, working to push back the enemies, ignorance or boredom. Neither force will give the other peace. Introduce a new piece of information and the organism immediately tries to connect it. When the organism has a connection, it seeks new information to reinforce it.

There is another pair of powerful countervailing forces at work at the same time that information is being collected and connected. The force with the primary thrust is *writing.* Man has a primitive need to write. Carol Chomsky (1971) tells us that children want to write, in fact need to write, before they want to read. And indeed someone had to write during the prelude to history; that person was also the first reader. We all have a primitive need to experience experience by articulating it. When we tell others or ourselves what has happened to us it makes that happening more real and often understandable. We need both to record and to share, both to talk to ourselves within the enormous room of the mind and to talk to others. Children—and some professors—think out loud; but for most of us, our speech is socially suppressed, done silently. Since we continue to talk to ourselves within the privacy of our skulls, some of that talking, if made public, is writing.

The act of voicing experience and connecting it involves, I think, fundamentally an aural facility. We record in written language what we say in our heads. This does not mean that writing is simply oral language written down. I believe we have a private speech we use when writing. When we know we may write, we silently practice expressing ourselves in our potential writing voices. Later we may record and revise in written language what sounded right when tried out in that silent voice within our minds. At least, this is how I think I write, dictating to myself, recording in written language what I have heard myself say milliseconds before. For many years I have dictated much of my nonfiction prose, but I was not aware until recently when I studied my own writing process that I listened to my voice while I wrote "silently" with typewriter or by pen.

Working against this powerful force of writing is the counterforce of *reading.* Put writing down on paper and it is read as it appears. Reading seems to involve criticism. We make comparisons; we look for immediate clarity, for instant grace. Just as connecting can control collecting too effectively and too early, so reading can suppress writing. The writer has to develop new forms of reading, to read loosely at first, to give the piece of writing space so that the embryonic patterns of meaning which are making shadowy appearance can have time to come clear. Writers have to learn to listen for the almost imperceptible sounds which may develop into the voice they do not expect. As the meanings come clear, the voices grow stronger. The writer has to read with increasing care, has to be critical, even surgical, but not at first.

These two forces work against each other almost simultaneously within the act of writing. In listening to the voices within our skull we "read" those voices and change them. As Perl (1979) has documented, we write and react to those marks on paper, continually testing the word against the experience, the word against the one before and the one to come next. Eventually, we extend the range of this testing to phrase, to sentence, to paragraph, to page. When I got bifocals, I had to buy lenses with an extra large reading area. They were strangely called "the executive model." But when I am writing I take them off and move my nose closer to the page. My eyes darting back and forth across my writing break out of the area bounded by my "executive" bifocals. In action writing, we do not make the separation of reading and writing that we make in school. We *writeread* or *readwrite.*

The forces of the writing process also relate to each other. This is indicated by the dotted line in the following diagram. The act of collecting is

also an act of writing and reading. We cannot collect information and store it without naming it and reading that name. We also connect information by using language, whereby symbols carry the information. It is language which often seems to direct us towards significant connections, and we are led to them by the acts of writing and reading.

The Forces: In Balance and Out

We must always remember that each writing act is a complex instantaneous interaction. The true diagram of the writing of a sentence might look like this.

If we can manage to survive that vision after multiplying it a thousand times or more for each draft of a short essay, then we may be able to see that there is a significant sequence of balance and imbalance which takes place while the forces interact during rehearsing, drafting, and revising. During rehearsing we must give writing and collecting a slight advantage, holding off the forces of criticism and order. In revising the opposite is true. We load the dice in favor of reading and connecting. We become more critical, more orderly. The advantage holds until the balance tips. When the advantage passes again to writing and collecting, then revising becomes rehearsing.

If we see how the balance works, the scale tipped toward discovery at one time and clarification at another, then we will come to a new definition of drafting. The draft occurs when the four forces are in tentative balance. The forces have worked against each other to produce a meaning which can be read and which could perhaps be published.

In the beginning of the writing process there is no draft because the forces are wildly out of balance. The imbalance will be different with different pieces of writing, but it is there. For example, language may race ahead to the point of incoherence or be just fragmentary, a matter of notes. There may be an abundance of information which is just a jumble—no order has yet appeared from it—or there may be merely a neat, precise order, a thesis statement and outline for which there is no documentation. The process of rehearsal, however, brings the forces into balance. The writing can be read; the information begins to assume a meaningful order. The draft emerges.

The writer thinks the task is finished, that the balance will hold. But when the writer turns to read the page, it becomes apparent that the language is too stiff, too clumsy, has no flow. The reader will not follow it. Or, there is too much information; the writing goes off on tangents. Material has to be cut out and reordered. The writer may be able to help the piece of writing find its meaning through a modest amount of rewriting and researching, reordering and rereading. But many times the imbalance gets worse. The piece of writing has to follow a tangent; a new major point has to be included. Or, in fact, the major point becomes the main point. New material has to be sought out and its order discovered. The piece of writing is severely out of balance and will be brought towards balance only by rehearsing. I think it may be helpful for us to think of drafts and a series of drafts in this way, for it helps us see what has to be done to encourage a piece of writing to find its own meaning.

Continued observation and reflection upon the writing process will result in new speculations. They will come because it is our desire, reinforced by our education, to connect, to make lists, charts, maps, to find patterns and orders. This tendency is appropriate. That is what our business is. But we must remind ourselves again and again that the writing process is a kinetic activity, a matter of instantaneous motion, action and reaction which is never still. There is no clear line between the stages of rehearsing, drafting, and revising. The most meaning-producing actions may, in fact, take place on the seams between these stages when the tensions between them is the greatest.

The same thing is true of the action between the forces. We do not collect and connect and then write the connection and then read it. These forces are in action against each other, and that action produces meaning. The calm, logical moment when the words stand at dress parade and present a meaning gives no hint of the battles which produce that moment—or the battles which may be ahead.

Teaching the Composing Process

In the preceding pages I have proposed a theory of how a piece of writing finds its own meaning. That theory has come out of practice. It is rooted in the experience of making meaning with written language. Theory, however, must return to practice in our field. A writing theory that can not be practiced by teachers, writers, or students and that does not produce increasingly effective drafts of writing must be reconsidered. We also have an obligation to show how the theory can be put into practice. We must show that our students are able to write more effectively and produce pieces of writing that find their own meaning because they understand what happens during the writing act. If we accept the process theory of teaching writing, then we must be able to suggest ways in which our students can experience the writing process.

In teaching the process we have to look, not at what students need to know, but what they need to experience. This separates the teaching of writing from the teaching of a course in which the content is produced by authorities —writers of literature, scientists, historians—and interpreted by textbooks and teachers. The writing teacher has no such content. It would be bizarre for the process teacher to deliver a lecture on the process theory of composition in advance of writing—just as bizarre as it would be to deliver a lecture on rhetoric, linguistics, grammar, or any other theoretical concepts before the student writes. Such information would be meaningless to the student. It might even be harmful because the student who hears such information without the perspective of his or her own experience can develop serous misconceptions about the writing process. For example, a student might get the dangerous misconception that writers know the form before they know the content, that students know what they have to say before they say it. I would not write—would not need to write—if I knew what I was going to say before I said it. I must help my students find out through a successful writing experience why that is true.

In the writing process approach, the teacher and student face the task of making meaning together. The task is ever new, for they share the blank page and an ignorance of purpose and of outcome. They start on a trip of exploration together. They find where they are going as they get there.

This requires of the writing teacher a special kind of courage. The teacher not only has to face blank papers but blank students worried by their blankness, and a blank curriculum which worries the teacher's supervisors. The teacher has to restrain himself or herself from providing a content, taking care not to inhibit the students from finding their own subjects, their own forms, and their own language.

The writing teacher who is writing and, therefore, knows how the stages in the writing process work and how the forces within that process interact, understands the students' natural desire for premature order expressed, in part, by the question, "What do you want?" The teacher must resist the impulse to respond with a prescription. It is better to explain to the students why their writing needs room—time and space—to find its own meaning.

The first day of the writing unit should begin with writing, not talking. The students write and the teacher writes. This beginning is, of course, a symbolic gesture. It demonstrates that the information in the course will come from the student. The students produce the principal text in the writing course.

It is very hard for traditionally-trained teachers who are not writing themselves to believe that students can write without instruction from the teacher or without assignment. Teachers often do not have enough faith in their students to feel that the students have anything to say. They also may not realize that much, perhaps most, of the poor writing they see in school is the product of the assignments they give. Most assignments I see guarantee bad writing. In many cases assignments direct students to write on subjects in which they have no interest and on which they have no information. They have to adopt a point of view implicit in the assignments or in the way teachers present them. They have to accept forms and perhaps languages which are not appropriate to their subjects—or their visions of the subjects.

Of course, students like assignments. Why not? They make things easy. The good students know instantly what the teacher wants; the poor students deliver as best they can. And neither group has to make a personal commitment to the writing.

It is important that the writing course which is built on the writing process set that process in action immediately. In fact, this approach might be called the writing/response method. The student writes, then the teacher and the class respond. One device I have used to begin a writing class is to hand out six 3 × 5 cards of different colors. I ask the students to take a card and brainstorm specific details about a person or place, or an event which was important to them. They may also just brainstorm random specifics. After three or four minutes I share my own list with the class. Then I ask them to circle a specific on their own cards which surprised them, or to connect two specifics with an unexpected relationship. I share my surprises with them. Then I tell them to take another card and start with that moment of surprise, or just start free writing. After three or four minutes I again share my writing with them and ask them to take another card, to continue on, start anew, or switch the point of view. And so we work through the cards. At the end we each share one card, reading it aloud without comment.

I have worked out all sorts of variations of this exercise, and so have teachers to whom I've introduced it. The important thing is that students write upon demand, that they write of what they know, that they are placed under enough pressure so they write what they did not expect to write, that the cards are small enough and switched frequently enough so they have a new chance if one doesn't go well, that the teacher shares his or her writing with them, that they listen to the voices which are coming from the members of *their* writing community, and that they discover that writing is a process of discovery.

Under such conditions I find that writing is produced. Nine hundred and ninety-nine students out of a thousand will write on demand. But if one doesn't write, not to worry. Writing is contagious. It is almost impossible to resist the desire to write in your own voice, of your own concerns, when you are part of a supportive writing community.

Sharing Writing

Once the writing is produced, it is shared. I have come to believe that this sharing, at least in the beginning, should be done orally. When students read their papers aloud they hear the voices of their classmates without the interference of mechanical problems, misspellings, and poor penmanship. Those problems will have to be dealt with in due time, but first the students—and especially the teacher—should hear the voices which come from the page.

It is equally important, perhaps more important, for the writer to hear his or her own voice. Our voices often tell us a great deal about the subject. The piece of writing speaks with its own voice of its own concerns, direction, meaning. The student writer hears that voice from the piece convey intensity, drive, energy, and more—anger, pleasure, happiness, sadness, caring, frustration, understanding, explaining. The meaning of a piece of writing comes from what it says *and* how it says it.

As the students in the writing class hear a piece of writing, they laugh with the author, grieve with the author, nod in understanding, lean forward to try to learn more. That's how the writing class begins, and that is what carries it forward. The community of writers instinctively understands that each piece of writing is trying to work its way towards a meaning. The community wants to help the writer help the piece of writing find its own meaning.

The experience of sharing writing should be reinforced by the writing conference. Individual conferences are the principal form of instruction in the writing process approach. As we have speculated upon the process by which a piece of writing finds its own meaning, we have seen how important it is to listen to the piece of writing and to pay attention to how that piece of writing is making itself heard. We must, in our conferences, help the student respect the piece of writing, pay attention to what it is trying to say, and experience the process of helping it say it.

We get the student to talk about the paper and to talk about the forces which produced the draft. We do this in conference, and we do it in workshop. I have come to believe that the workshop works best when it begins with a public conference between the writer and the teacher. The teacher gives the student the opportunity to talk about the piece of writing—what the student sees in it, what technical problems the student identifies, what questions the student has for the readers—and encourages the student to talk about the process by which the writing is being produced. The teacher initiates the conference, but soon the class joins in, writers helping writers listen to the evolving writing.

There are few lectures and large group exercises—if any—in the writing class. What is there to say until a draft is heard? Who can predict the proper response to an event which has not taken place? There are, in fact, no classes; there are workshops in which writing is shared. The writers in the workshop study drafts in process to see what meanings are evolving and, thereby, learn to anticipate what may appear on the page as well as read what has appeared.

In my own workshops I publish only the best work. The most effective teaching occurs when the students who have produced that work talk about how they have produced it. This is when I am able to show students what they have learned, and by so doing I constantly learn with them.

> How were you able to get a first draft to work so well?
> Well, I don't know. It just seemed to go together.
> Well, what did you do before you started to write?
> Not much. I didn't make an outline or anything.
> Did you think much about the piece of writing you were going to do?
> Oh yeah, sure. I think about it all the time, trying out different things, you know, like what you're going to say at the party, or to the girl. Stuff like that, kinda' practicing in your head.

And we're into a discussion of rehearsal as I get this student, and others, to tell about how they do this in their minds and on their pages. I underline, extend, reinforce, and teach what at least some of them have already done so that they know what they've done and may be able to apply it to other writing tasks. Others in the class who have not tried it are encouraged to try it in the future.

This is the way the writing unit unwinds. The attitudes appropriate to rehearsing, drafting, and revising are expressed in conferences and in class by the students and the teacher. The skills of rehearsing, drafting, and revising are refined after they have worked successfully on an evolving draft. Concurrently, the forces of *reading* and *writing, collecting* and *connecting* are identified. The students and the teacher share their techniques for developing and controlling these forces, for helping to bring them into effective balance.

The greatest hazard for the teacher is the natural tendency not to respect the forces and instead to supply the student with the teacher's information, to make the teacher's connection, to use the teacher's language, to read what the teacher sees in the text. The teacher must remember, in workshop and in conference, to stand back and give the student room so that the student can give the writing room to find its own meaning. The teacher should not look at the text for the student, not even with the student. The teacher looks at—and listens to—the student watching the text evolve.

The teacher is not coy and does not withhold information that the student needs. But the teacher must practice the patience and restraint of the writer. The writer treats the evolving drafts with respect, trying to help the piece of writing work towards its own meaning. The teacher demonstrates this attitude by treating the student with respect so that the student will respect his or her own evolving writing. By asking helpful questions of the student, the teacher shows the student how to question his or her own drafts: "What did you learn from this piece of writing?" "Where is the piece of writing taking you?" "What do you feel works best in this piece of writing?"

Evaluation of Writing

I am always amused when people feel that a writing course is permissive, that anything goes, that there is no serious evaluation. The fact is there is much more evaluation in the writing course than in the traditional content course. Evaluation in the writing course is not a matter of an occasional test. As the student passes through the stages of the writing process and tries to bring the forces within the process into balance, there is constant evaluation of the writing in process.

This evaluation begins with each word as it is considered and reconsidered in the mind and then as it appears on the paper. The word is reevaluated as the phrase is created and recorded. The phrase is reevaluated as the sentence is created and recorded. The sentence is reevaluated as the paragraph is created and recorded. The paragraph is reevaluated as the page is created and recorded. The page is reevaluated as the entire piece of writing is created and recorded. And then the writer, having once finished the writing and put it away, picks it up and evaluates it again.

In the writing course the writer's evaluation is shared with the teacher or with other writers in the class. The evaluation is evaluated as the writing itself is evaluated. For example:

I don't like the writing at all in this draft. It's gross.

You think it's all gross?

Yeah.

Well, I don't think it's all gross. Some of it may be gross, but what do you think is less gross?

Well, I suppose that description of how to start the snowmobile works pretty well.

Yes, that piece of writing seems to know what it's doing. Why do you think it does?

Well, it seems to be lined up pretty well. I mean, like it goes along, sort of natural.

That's how it seems to me.

Think maybe I should make the rest try to work that way? It's kind of jumbled up now.

Try it if you want.

Each draft, often each part of the draft, is discussed with readers—the teacher-writer and the other student-writers. Eventually the writing is published in a workshop, and a small or large group of readers evaluate it. It is evaluated on many levels. Is there a subject? Does it say anything? Is it worth saying? Is it focused? Is it documented? Is it ordered? Are the parts developed? Is the writing clear? Does it have an appropriate voice? Do the sentences work? Do the paragraphs work? Are the verbs strong? Are the nouns specific? Is the spelling correct? Does the punctuation clarify?

There is, in fact, so much evaluation, so much self-criticism, so much rereading, that the writing teacher has to help relieve the pressure of criticism to make sure that the writer has a bearable amount. The pressure must be there, but it never should be so great that it creates paralysis or destroys self-respect. Effective writing depends on the student's respect for the potential that may appear. The student has to have faith in the evolving draft to be able to see its value. To have faith in the draft means having faith in the self.

The teacher by the very nature of the writing course puts enormous pressure on the student. There are deadlines. The student will write every day. Over my desk hangs the exhortation "nulla dies sine linea," never a day without a line, which is attributed to Pliny and which has hung over Trollope's writing desk and Updike's. I give copies of it to my students, and I practice it myself. There should, in the writing unit, be at least weekly deadlines. There is an unrelenting demand for writing.

Writing means self-exposure. No matter how objective the tone or how detached the subject, the writer is exposed by words on the page. It is natural for students and for writers to fear such exposure. That fear can be relieved best if the writer, the fellow students, and the teacher look together at the piece of writing to see what the piece of writing is saying, and if they listen to the piece of writing with appropriate detachment.

When we write, we confront ourselves, but we also confront our subject. In writing the drafts of this chapter, "How Writing Finds Its Own Meaning," I found meanings I did not expect. I suppose that I was invited to do this chapter because of the definitions and the descriptions of the writing process I have published in the past. I accepted the invitation because I had completed a new description which has since been published elsewhere. But in the months that it has taken me to help this piece of writing find its own meaning I have found new meanings. This is not the chapter I intended to write. The process described here is different from what I have described before. This piece of writing revolted against my intent and taught me what I did not know.

By the time this is published I will, I hope, have moved on. There are those who may be concerned by what they consider inconsistency or disloyalty to my own words. No matter, I have no choice. The pieces of writing I have not yet thought of writing will become different from what I expect them to be when I propose them to myself. My constant is change. My teaching changes from year to year and day to day. I do not teach my students what I have learned in the past. My students teach themselves what we are learning together.

Those of us who teach the writing process are comfortable with the constant change. This sets us apart from many people in the academic world who teach in a traditional or classical mode, believing there are truths which can be learned and passed on from teacher to student, from generation to generation. Their conception has its attractions; it is the one I was taught. But my life as a writer and as a teacher of writing leads me—as similar experience has led others—to a different tradition which some call developmental or truly humanistic. We do not teach our students rules demonstrated by static models; we teach our students to write by allowing them to experience the process of writing. That is a process of discovery, of using written language to find out what we have to say. We believe this process can be adapted by our students to whatever writing tasks face them—the memo, the poem, the textbook, the speech, the consumer complaint, the job application, the story, the essay, the personal letter, the movie script, the accident report, the novel, the scientific paper. There is no way we can tell what our students will need to write in their lives beyond the classroom, but we can give our students a successful experience in the writing process. We can let them discover how writing finds its own meaning.

While editing this collection I'm in the middle of a research project in which I'm serving as a laboratory rat for Carol Berkenkotter of Michigan Technological University, for whom I'm supplying naturalistic writing protocols. Her work has made clear to me how important and extensive are those activities we usually lump under the term prewriting.

It's easier to research those writing activities which produce a completed text or revise and edit a completed text, but the quality of the text, I'm convinced, depends largely on what my colleague, Donald Graves, calls *rehearsal.* And I expect that the focus of much of my work in the immediate future will be to try to explore in more detail the territory I attempted to stake out in the following article.

5
Write Before Writing

We command our students to write and grow frustrated when our "bad" students hesitate, stare out the window, dawdle over blank paper, give up and say, "I can't write," while the "good" students smugly pass their papers in before the end of the period.

When publishing writers visit such classrooms, however, they are astonished at students who can write on command, ejaculating correct little essays without thought, for writers have to write before writing.

The writers were the students who dawdled, stared out windows, and, more often than we like to admit, didn't do well in English—or in school.

One reason may be that few teachers have ever allowed adequate time for prewriting, that essential stage in the writing process which precedes a completed first draft. And even the curricula plans and textbooks which attempt to deal with prewriting usually pass over it rather quickly referring only to the techniques of outlining, note-taking, or journal-making, not revealing the complicated process writers work through to get to the first draft.

Writing teachers, however, should give careful attention to what happens between the moment the writer receives an idea or an assignment and the moment the first completed draft is begun. We need to understand, as well as

Published in *College Composition and Communication,* December, 1978.

we can, the complicated and intertwining processes of perception and conception through language.

In actual practice, of course, these stages overlap and interact with one another, but to understand what goes on we must separate them and look at them artificially, the way we break down any skill to study it.

First of all, we must get out of the stands where we observe the process of writing from a distance—and after the fact—and get on the field where we can understand the pressures under which the writer operates. On the field, we will discover there is one principal negative force which keeps the writer from writing and four positive forces which help the writer move forward to a completed draft.

Resistance to Writing

The negative force is *resistance* to writing, one of the great natural forces of nature. It may be called The Law of Delay: that writing which can be delayed, will be. Teachers and writers too often consider resistance to writing evil, when, in fact, it is necessary.

When I get an idea for a poem or an article or a talk or a short story, I feel myself consciously draw away from it. I seek procrastination and delay. There must be time for the seed of the idea to be nurtured in the mind. Far better writers than I have felt the same way. Over his writing desk Franz Kafka had one word, "Wait." William Wordsworth talked of the writer's "wise passiveness." Naturalist Annie Dillard recently said, "I'm waiting. I usually get my ideas in November, and I start writing in January. I'm waiting." Denise Levertov says, "If...somewhere in the vicinity there is a poem, then, no, I don't do anything about it, I wait."

Even the most productive writers are expert dawdlers, doers of unnecessary errands, seekers of interruptions—trials to their wives or husbands, friends, associates, and themselves. They sharpen well-pointed pencils and go out to buy more blank paper, rearrange offices, wander through libraries and bookstores, chop wood, walk, drive, make unnecessary calls, nap, daydream, and try not "consciously" to think about what they are going to write so they can think subconsciously about it.

Writers fear this delay, for they can name colleagues who have made a career of delay, whose great unwritten books will never be written, but, somehow, those writers who write must have the faith to sustain themselves through the necessity of delay.

Forces for Writing

In addition to that faith, writers feel four pressures that move them forward towards the first draft.

The first is *increasing information* about the subject. Once a writer decides on a subject or accepts an assignment, information about the subject seems to attach itself to the writer. The writer's perception apparatus finds significance in what the writer observes or overhears or reads or thinks or remembers. The writer becomes a magnet for specific details, insights, anecdotes, statistics, connecting thoughts, references. The subject itself seems to take hold of the writer's experience, turning everything that happens to the writer into material. And this inventory of information creates pressure that moves the writer forward towrad the first draft.

Usually the writer feels an *increasing concern* for the subject. The more a writer knows about the subject, the more the writer begins to feel about the subject. The writer cares that the subject be ordered and shared. The concern, which at first is a vague interest in the writer's mind, often becomes an obsession until it is communicated. Winston Churchill said, ''Writing a book was an adventure. To begin with, it was a toy and amusement; then it became a mistress, and then a master. And then a tyrant.''

The writer becomes aware of a *waiting audience,* potential readers who want or need to know what what the writer has to say. Writing is an act of arrogance and communication. The writer rarely writes just for himself or herself, but for others who may be informed, entertained, or persuaded by what the writer has to say.

And perhaps most important of all, is the *approaching deadline,* which moves closer day by day at a terrifying and accelerating rate. Few writers publish without deadlines, which are imposed by others or by themselves. The deadline is real, absolute, stern, and commanding.

Rehearsal for Writing

What the writer does under the pressure not to write and the four countervailing pressures to write is best described by the word *rehearsal,* which I first heard used by Dr. Donald Graves of the University of New Hampshire to describe what he saw young children doing as they began to write. He watched them draw what they would write and heard them, as we all have, speaking aloud what they might say on the page before they wrote. If you walk through editorial offices or a newspaper cityroom you will see lips moving and hear expert professionals muttering and whispering to themselves as they write. Rehearsal is a normal part of the writing process, but it took a trained observer such as Dr. Graves, to identify its significance.

Rehearsal covers much more than the muttering of struggling writers. As Dr. Graves points out, productive writers are ''in a state of rehearsal all the time.'' Rehearsal usually begins with an unwritten dialogue within the writer's mind. ''All of a sudden I discover what I have been thinking about a play,'' says Edward Albee. ''This is usually between six months and a year before I actually sit down and begin typing it out.'' The writer thinks about characters or arguments, about plot or structure, about words and lines. The writer usually hears something which is similar to what Wallace Stevens must have heard as he walked through his insurance office working out poems in his head.

What the writer hears in his or her head usually evolves into note-taking. This may be simple brainstorming, the jotting down of random bits of information which may connect themselves into a pattern later on, or it may be journal-writing, a written dialogue between the writer and the subject. It may even become research recorded in a formal structure of note-taking.

Sometimes the writer not only talks to himself or herself, but to others—collaborators, editors, teachers, friends—working out the piece of writing in oral language with someone else who can enter into the process of discovery with the writer.

For most writers, the informal notes turn into lists, outlines, titles, leads, ordered fragments, all sketches of what later may be written, devices to catch a possible order that exists in the chaos of the subject.

In the final stage of rehearsal, the writer produces test drafts, written or unwritten. Sometimes they are called discovery drafts or trial runs or false starts that the writer doesn't think will be false. All writing is experimental, and the writer must come to the point where drafts are attempted in the writer's head and on paper.

Some writers seem to work more in their head, and others more on paper. Susan Sowers, a researcher at the University of New Hampshire, examining the writing processes of a group of graduate students found

> a division . . . between those who make most discoveries during pre-writing and those who make most discoveries during writing and revision. The discoveries include the whole range from insights into personal issues to task-related organizational and content insight. The earlier the stage at which insights occur, the greater the drudgery associated with the writing-rewriting tasks. It may be that we resemble the young reflective and reactive writers. The less developmentally mature reactive writers enjoy writing more than reflective writers. They may use writing as a rehearsal for thinking just as young, reactive writers draw to rehearse writing. The younger and older reflective writers do not need to rehearse by drawing to write or by writing to think clearly or to discover new relationships and significant content.

This concept deserves more investigation. We need to know about both the reflective and reactive prewriting mode. We need to see if there are developmental changes in students, if they move from one mode to another as they mature, and we need to see if one mode is more important in certain writing tasks than others. We must, in every way possible, explore the significant writing stage of rehearsal which has rarely been described in the literature on the writing process.

The Signals Which Say "Write"

During the rehearsal process, the experienced writer sees signals which tell the writer how to control the subject and produce a working first draft. The writer, Rebecca Rule, points out that in some cases when the subject is found, the way to deal with it is inherent in the subject. The subject itself is the signal. Most writers have experienced this quick passing through of the prewriting process. The line is given and the poem is clear; a character gets up and walks the writer through the story; the newspaperman attends a press conference, hears a quote, sees the lead and the entire structure of the article instantly. But many times the process is far less clear. The writer is assigned a subject or chooses one and then is lost.

E. B. White testifies, "I never knew in the morning how the day was going to develop. I was like a hunter hoping to catch sight of a rabbit." Denise Levertov says, "You can smell the poem before you see it." Most writers know these feelings but students who have never seen a rabbit dart across their writing desks or smelled a poem need to know the signals which tell them that a piece of writing is near.

What does the writer recognize which gives a sense of closure, a way of handling a diffuse and overwhelming subject? There seem to be eight principal signals to which writers respond.

One signal is *genre.* Most writers view the world as a fiction writer, a reporter, a poet, or an historian. The writer sees experience as a plot or a lyric poem or a news story or a chronicle. The writer uses such literary traditions to see and understand life.

"Ideas come to a writer because he has trained his mind to seek them out," says Brian Garfield. "Thus when he observes or reads or is exposed to a character or event, his mind sees the story possibilities in it and he begins to compose a dramatic structure in his mind. This process is incessant. Now and then it leads to something that will become a novel. But it's mainly an attitude: a way of looking at things; a habit of examining everything one perceives as potential material for a story."

Genre is a powerful but dangerous lens. It both clarifies and limits. The writer and the student must be careful not to see life merely in the stereotype form with which he or she is most familiar but to look at life with all of the possibilities of the genre in mind and to attempt to look at life through different genre.

Another signal the writer looks for is a *point of view.* This can be an opinion towards the subject or a position from which the writer—and the reader—studies the subject.

A tenement fire could inspire the writer to speak out against tenements, dangerous space-heating system, a fire-department budget cut. The fire might also be seen from the point of view of the people who were the victims or who escaped or who came home to find their home gone. It may be told from the point of view of a fireman, an arsonist, an insurance investigator, a fire-safety engineer, a real-estate planner, a housing inspector, a landlord, a spectator, as well as the victim. The list could go on.

Still another way the writer sees the subject is through *voice.* As the writer rehearses, in the writer's head and on paper, the writer listens to the sound of the language as a clue to the meaning of the subject and the writer's attitude toward that meaning. Voice is often the force which drives a piece of writing forward, which illuminates the subject for the writer and the reader.

A writer may, for example, start to write a test draft with detached unconcern and find that the language appearing on the page reveals anger or passionate concern. The writer who starts to write a solemn report of a meeting may hear a smile and then a laugh in his own words and go on to produce a humorous column.

News is an important signal for many writers who ask what the reader needs to know or would like to know. Those prolific authors of nature books, Lorus and Margery Milne, organize their books and each chapter in the books around what is new in the field. Between assignment and draft they are constantly looking for the latest news they can pass along to their readers. When they find what is new, then they know how to organize their writing.

Writers constantly wait for the *line* which is given. For most writers, there is an enormous difference between a thesis or an idea or a concept and an actual line, for the line itself has resonance. A single line can imply a voice, a tone, a pace, a whole way of treating a subject. Joseph Heller tells about the signal which produced his novel *Something Happened.*

> I begin with a first sentence that is independent of any conscious preparation. Most often nothing comes out of it: a sentence will come to mind that doesn't lead to a second sentence. Sometimes it will lead to thirty sentences which then come to a dead end. I was alone on the deck. As I sat there worrying and wondering what to do, one of those first lines suddenly came to mind: "In the office in which I work, there are four people of whom I am afraid. Each of these four people is afraid of five people." Immediately, the lines presented a whole explosion of possibilities and choices—characters (working in a corporation), a tone, a mood of anxiety, or of insecurity. In that first hour (before someone came along and asked me to go to the beach) I knew the beginning, the ending, most of the middle, the whole scene of that particular "something" that was going to happen; I knew about the brain-damaged child, and especially, of course, about Bob Slocum, my protagonist, and what frightened him, that he wanted to be liked, that his immediate hope was to be allowed to make a three-minute speech at the company convention. Many of the actual lines throughout the book came to me—the entire "something happened" scene with those solar plexus lines (beginning with the doctor's statement and ending with "Don't tell my wife" and the rest of them) all coming to me in the first hour on that Fire Island deck. Eventually I found a different opening chapter with a different first line ("I get the willies when I see closed doors") but I kept the original which had spurred everything to start off the second section.

Newspapermen are able to write quickly and effectively under pressure because they become skillful at identifying a lead, that first line—or two or three—which will inform and entice the reader and which, of course, also gives the writer control over the subject. As an editorial writer, I found that finding the title first gave me control over the subject. Each title became, in effect, a pre-draft, so that in listing potential titles I would come to one which would be a signal as to how the whole editorial could be written.

Poets and fiction writers often receive their signals in terms of an *image.* Sometimes this image is static; other times it is a moving picture in the writer's mind. When Gabriel Garcia Marquez was asked what the starting point of his novels was, he answered, "A completely visual image . . . the starting point of *Leaf Storm* is an old man taking his grandson to a funeral, in *No One Writes to the Colonel,* it's an old man waiting, and in *One Hundred Years,* an old man taking his grandson to the fair to find out what ice is." William Faulkner was quoted as saying, "It begins with a character, usually, and once he stand up on his feet and begins to move, all I do is trot along behind him with a paper and pencil trying to keep up long enough to put down what he says and does." It's a comment which seems facetious—if you're not a fiction writer. Joyce Carol Oates adds, "I visualize the characters completely; I have heard their dialogue, I know how they speak, what they want, who they are, nearly everything about them."

Although image has been testified to mostly by imaginative writers, where it is obviously most appropriate, I think research would show that nonfiction writers often see an image as the signal. The person, for example, writing a memo about a manufacturing procedure may see the assembly line in his or her mind. The politician arguging for a pension law may see a person robbed of a pension, and by seeing that person know how to organize a speech or the draft of a new law.

Many writers know they are ready to write when they see a *pattern* in a subject. This pattern is usually quite different from what we think of as an outline, which is linear and goes from beginning to end. Usually the writer sees something which might be called a gestalt, which is, in the world of the dictionary, "a unified physical, psychological, or symbolic configuration having properties that cannot be derived from its parts." The writer usually in a moment sees the entire piece of writing as a shape, a form, something that is more than all of its parts, something that is entire and is represented in his or her mind, and probably on paper, by a shape.

Marge Piercy says, "I think that the beginning of fiction, of the story, has to do with the perception of pattern in event." Leonard Gardner, in talking of his fine novel *Fat City,* said, "I had a definite design in mind. I had a sense of circle . . . of closing the circle at the end." John Updike says, "I really begin with some kind of solid, coherent image, some notion of the shape of the book and even of its texture. *The Poorhouse Fair* was meant to have a sort of wide shape. *Rabbit, Run* was kind of zigzag. *The Centaur* was sort of a sandwich."

We have interviews with imaginative writers about the writing process, but rarely interviews with science writers, business writers, political writers, journalists, ghost writers, legal writers, medical writers—examples of effective writers who use language to inform and persuade. I am convinced that such research would reveal that they also see patterns or gestalts which carry them from idea to draft.

"It's not the answer that enlightens but the question," says Ionesco. This insight into what the writer is looking for is one of the most significant considerations in trying to understand the free-writing process. A most significant book based on more than ten years of study of art students, *The Creative Vision, A Longitudinal Study of Problem-Finding in Art,* by Jacob W. Getzels and Mihaly Csikszentmihalyi, has documented how the most creative students are those who come up with the *problem* to be solved rather than a quick answer. The signal to the creative person may well be the problem, which will be solved through the writing.

We need to take all the concepts of invention from classical rhetoric and combine them with what we know from modern psychology, from studies of creativity, from writers' testimony about the prewriting process. Most of all, we need to observe successful students and writers during the prewriting process, and to debrief them to find out what they do when they move effectively from assignment or idea to completed first draft. Most of all, we need to move from failure-centered research to research which defines what happens when the writing goes well, just what is the process followed by effective student and professional writers. We know far too little about the writing process.

Implications for Teaching Writing

Our speculations make it clear that there are significant implications for the teaching of writing in a close examination of what happens between receiving an assignment or finding a subject and beginning a completed first draft. We may need, for example, to reconsider our attitude toward those who delay writing. We may, in fact, need to force many of our glib, hair-trigger student writers to slow down, to daydream, to waste time, but not to avoid a reasonable deadline.

We certainly should allow time within the curriculum for prewriting, and we should work with our students to help them understand the process of rehearsal, to allow them the experience of rehearsing what they will write in their minds, on the paper, and with collaborators.

We should also make our students familiar with the signals they may see during the rehearsal process which will tell them that they are ready to write, that they have a way of dealing with their subject.

The prewriting process is largely invisible; it takes place within the writer's head or on scraps of paper that are rarely published. But we must understand that such a process takes place, that it is significant, and that it can be made clear to our students. Students who are not writing, or not writing well, may have a second chance if they are able to experience the writers' counsel to write before writing.

In academic writing the student writes for an audience of one. That audience knows the subject better than the writer and is also required to read what is written. Nonacademic writing is considerably different. The writer is the authority, and the reader is *not* required to read. The student will usually learn best in situations which reproduce the conditions of nonacademic writing. When faced with the challenge to become an authority and to capture the attention of an inattentive reader, it helps to know "what makes readers read."

6
What Makes Readers Read?

There seem to be five principal elements which make readers read. These forces work together and against each other to provide the excitement and satisfaction we find in readable writing.

Information. Readers hunger for specific information. The more concrete and detailed the information, the more it will interest readers who delight in facts, statistics, brief quotations, precise descriptions which satisfy the readers' curiosity, give the impression of authority, and provide readers with information they can pass on to someone else. The writer must satisfy the readers' appetite for specifics, but the writer should also be responsible and make sure the specifics are accurate and used in an appropriate context.

Significance. Readers want to know the meaning of the information they read and how it affects them. They are particularly interested when the writer reveals surprising connections between pieces of information. These connections make the biggest impact when readers recognize the significance of a connection they felt but had not articulated themselves.

People. Readers want to see people on the page, hear them talk, watch them in dramatic action and reaction with other people. They like to read anecdotes, the little scenes in which people reveal both themselves and the subject. Readers want to meet people with whom they can identify, and often readers become, for a few moments, the person on the page, and so extend their

Published in *English Journal,* May, 1979.

experience by living another life. Readers also enjoy a strong sense of place and time; they like to see the people they read about in their world—to be shown as well as told.

Order. Readers enjoy writing which has a firmly built structure and provides them with a sense of order. Reading is satisfying because, as Frost said of poetry, it provides "a momentary stay against confusion." Writing gives shape to experience. A piece of well-built writing may have many shapes—narrative, problem and solution, dominant impression, chronology, argument; a dozen different external or internal rhetorical forms—but the form itself is satisfying to the reader. Readers want writing to have resolution, a sense a completion. Above all, readers' questions must be anticipated and answered in a well-made piece of writing.

Voice. Readers respond to the voice of the writer, one individual speaking to another individual. Writing is not speech written down, but writing which is widely read gives the impression it is spoken. Readers pay attention to a voice which has authority, concern, and energy. Authority comes from a convincing command of information; concern comes from caring expressed through opinion or point of view; energy from language which is clear and honest, driven by verbs and sparked by the tension between ordinary words which reveals extraordinary meanings.

The work I've done with Carol Berkenkotter in studying my own writing process confirms what I've discovered as an observer of other writers, a teaching consultant to writers on professional publications, and a teacher of beginning and advanced students. The affective conditions—the environment and the feelings of the writer—usually control the writing act. Writing is only in part a cognitive activity. We must also describe, explore, and share the feelings that extend and limit the act of writing.

7
The Feel of Writing - and Teaching Writing

Emptiness. There will be no more words. Blackness. No, white without color. Silence.

I have not put down any words all day.It is late, and I am tired in the bone. I sit on the edge of the bed, open the notebook, uncap the pen. Nothing.

Or.

Everything has gone well this morning. I wake from sleep, not dreams, the car does not have a flat tire, I do not spill the coffee grounds, I do not turn the shower to cold instead of hot. The telephone does not ring, and I sit at the typewriter with a clean piece of white paper twirled into the machine. Nothing.

If I can make myself wait, remain calm, ready to write but not forcing writing, then words come out of silence. Out of nothing comes writing.

Now it is hard to keep up with the words which write what I did not intend, do not expect. Often this is the best writing, and I know it, but I never welcome that emptiness, that terrible feeling that there will be no more words.

• • •

The student sits in my conference chair, a Van Gogh miner, his hands clasped and hanging down between his legs near the floor, his head slumped forward. He mumbles. "I didn't write nothing." His head rolls up, his face

Reprinted from *Reinventing the Rhetorical Tradition,* edited by Aviva Freedman and Ian Pringle (Conway, AR: L & S Books, for the Canadian Council of Teachers of English, 1980), copyright by the Canadian Council of Teachers of English and reprinted by permission.

defiant, and then angry when he sees me smiling at him. "What's the matter?" he snarls.

"You look like me, sound like me this morning. Nothing happened."

"What d'ya do?"

"I wanted to kick the cat, but I don't have a cat, and I couldn't pick a fight with my wife. She was out shopping. So I had to sit there and wait."

"And?"

"The words came. Not what I expected. But words. You want to read them?"

I wait while he reads my uneven, early morning draft. I can see him getting interested and suspect he's saying to himself that he could do as good, or perhaps a bit better.

"You just wait?"

"Yes, it isn't easy though."

"Will it work for me?"

"I don't know. Sometimes it works for me and sometimes it doesn't."

• • •

The writing is going well. Everything is connecting. I need a word, and it is in my ear; I need a fact, and it flows out of my fingers; I need a more effective order, and my eye watches sentences as they rearrange themselves on the page. I think this is what writing should be like, and then I stop. I go for another mug of coffee, visit the bathroom, check the mail.

I wonder about this compulsion to interrupt writing which is going well. I see my students do it in the writing workshop. It's so much of a pattern there must be a reason for it. Sometimes I think it is the workman's need to stand back to get distance; other times I think it is simple Calvinist distrust—when everything's going well something must be wrong.

• • •

My students arrive in class just at the bell, as if they were hurled there by some gleeful giant. They are rushed, harried, driven. They remind me of me. I barely made it myself. How am I going to create a quiet space around us within which we can listen to writing trying to find its voice?

This is the writer's problem: take all the energy you have to fight your way to the writing desk: reject wife, child, friend, colleague, neighbor; refuse to carry out the trash, take the car to the garage, transplant the blueberry bush; leave the mail unopened and the opened mail unanswered; let the telephone ring; do not answer the knock on the door or prepare for class; ignore the message on your desk to call somebody back; do not rehearse the speech that will impress at the afternoon meeting; do not remember, do not plan; use all your energy to get to your desk, and then try to sit there, calmly, serenely, listening for writing.

I hear a teacher asking a student who has just begun to write, "What is your purpose?"

I hope the teacher will not come to my door when I have just begun to write. What, indeed, is my purpose? To make it through the day? To get tenure? (I already have tenure.) To become rich? (I will not eat on this article.) To impress my parents? (That sounds more like it, but they are dead, and would not read what I wrote when they were alive because, true Scots, they knew they would be disappointed.)

I hear more of the teacher's questions. "What is your purpose in this piece? What do you intend to say in the piece you are writing? Who is your audience?" They may be good questions but it's the first week of the semester and the student has passed in his first tentative draft.

He'd better not ask me. If I knew all those things—my purpose, my content, my reader—I wouldn't have to write this. Well, that's not really true. Perhaps I know my audience in a sort of general way, and perhaps I know what I'm going to say. And that worries me, because I want to write to surprise myself. It would be terrible if I knew my purpose, if I knew what I was doing, how it would all come out. That's when I'll know I'm finished. There are few things more dangerous in writing than too much purpose.

• • •

The mind's eye is real. I do not think up a scene in a novel; I watch it as you watch a movie, in living color, stereophonic sound, Panavision. I watch it and put down a little of what I see, enough to make your mind's eye see your own movie, knowing it will be different from mine.

• • •

Sometimes I come to my desk filled with an enormous impatience, a rage to get writing. I can't erase the image of a clumsy Holstein staggering, dragging herself back to the barn, her udder almost bounding on the ground she needs so badly to be milked.

Sometimes I think we should try to keep our students from writing. Get them started on a subject which is of deep personal importance to them, let them sense an audience in the class waiting to hear what they have to say, let them hear just a phrase or two of the voice they didn't know they had, then just try to stop them from writing. You can't stop me. My head will explode with writing. I must write. Now.

• • •

My students take their work far too seriously. They want to complete their papers the way they think I want them to complete them. What do you want, they keep asking me. They are so damned earnest, so excessively responsible. I want them to do what I do not expect them to do, and if they do not do what I do not expect them to do I must be failing somewhere.

It is the larger responsibility of the writer to be irresponsible, to play with the truths of his or her life, to put together what doesn't seem to belong together, to make connections which sever previous connections, to use language in ways that language can't seem to be used so that the act of writing will lead the writer to unexpected meanings.

• • •

The inspiration for writing lies within the work. I do not feel like writing when I come to my desk, but then language begins to move under my pen. It is alive, and I cannot help but watch it because it is the piece of writing which instructs me. The sound of the writing, its shape, its pace, its direction, its emerging form tells me what its meaning may be.

• • •

I start to get angry at the student sitting beside my desk. I have so many good and important things to say about the fine piece of work he has turned in. He looks by my head out the window at the tree and beyond. He has no interest in this piece of writing, which is no longer his, but mine. I end the conference. Relieved, he leaves.

Watching his escape I realize how unimportant publishing has become for me. It was something once important, something I had to do to be able to say to myself—and others—that I was a writer. The student is smarter than I was. Praise can cause more trouble than criticism. I began to like publication better than writing, but now I've gotten back to the joy in writing.

The doing is always more important than the done. I will publish it because it is something I do. It is expected of me. But there is no excitement in it. It is so far removed from the act of making that I cannot connect myself with the page that comes back to me through the mail. I see my name in a book, but the person who wrote that is a stranger now. The piece of writing on my desk is what concerns me.

I suppose publication is, at this time in my life, what marriage has become for most people these days, merely a public admission of what was done in private a long time before.

• • •

My father died with a machine plugged into his chest and a small smile on his face. The police found my mother on the floor of her apartment in a nest of covers tugged from the bed. My daughter, Lee, stands always at the corner of my eye, but at twenty she lay in a hospital bed, a beautiful woman without brainwaves. I made the decision to kill my father, to kill my mother, to kill my daughter, to let them go. I hope they have found more peace than I.

I have never said these words until this moment. I did not know I would say these words. They came out of silence. I heard them and I believe them.

Facing their own silences, my students write of death, of hate, of love, of living, of loss. They put down words which reveal a mother plunging a knife into a father while a girl looks on; a student tells of a failure—to kill herself; another student carries her father in her arms, rocking him, trying to comfort him against the pain of cancer in the night.

I tell them that they do not have to write of these things. I tell them they should write of such matters if it bothers them. They tell me it feels good, and then look guilty. I tell them I know. It helps, somehow, to put words on paper. I tell them it gives me distance, in a way, it makes what cannot be believed, a fact. I tell them I cannot understand why it feels good to write of such terrible things, but I confess it does feel good that is my way of achieving a kind of sanity.

• • •

A student comes to conference and shows me her new notebook. We marvel over it—a looseleaf notebook has a third arm with a clipboard on it which folds over the notebook. We share our wonder at it, for we share the thrill of writing and know the importance of tools. We are always trying out each other's pens or feeling the texture of a new kind of paper between our fingers. We are writers and we know that there is writing in the paper if we know how to let it out.

• • •

Often I write by not writing. I assign a task to my subconscious, then take a nap or go for a walk, do errands, and let my mind work on the problem. It doesn't do much good for me to think thinking.

I tell my students to write every day, for a short time, going away from it and coming back. The going away is as important as coming back. Read, stare out the window, jog, watch a ballgame, eat, go to bed. Sometimes I feel I have to make a note. It's too bad; for what can be forgotten usually should be forgotten. Writing surfaces from my subconscious, but I push it away, the way I shove an over-friendly puppy from my knee. Go away and work by yourself, writing, and come back when I'm at my desk.

• • •

I can recognize my students' papers without looking at their names. I hope they hear their own voices as clearly as I do, for writing is mostly a matter of listening. I sit at my desk listening to hear what my voice says within my head. Sometimes it speaks so clearly I feel I am taking down dictation while I write.

Voice gives writing the sense of an individual speaking to an individual. The reader wants to hear a voice. Voice carries the piece of writing forward; it glues the piece of writing together. Voice gives writing intensity and rhythm and humor and anger and sincerity and sadness. It is often the voice of a piece of writing that tells the writer what the writing means.

• • •

The experience I imagine, the one I have dreamt by writing, is often more real than the experience I have lived. I hope my students feel the twice-lived life of the writer, know the double experience of this kind of living.

• • •

Dictating this I pace the floor. I have just moved one chair and two rugs. Writing gives me so much energy it is hard for me to sit still. I move from one part of the room to the other, sit in this chair, leap up and move over to the couch. I stretch while I type, swing around in the chair, get up to pace and return. If I write by hand I work at the desk, then in the Morris chair on a lap desk, then over the rocker, then back to the desk, over to the couch. I encourage my students to move around in the writing workshop, to pace, twitch, mutter to themselves, hurl paper into the wastebasket. I can't write in libraries. My ideal work place is a bustling lunchroom in a town where no one knows me.

• • •

I don't want to know the rules of language. My problem is that my words discover rules all the time. My sentences obey rules I don't even know. One problem in writing is that my students and I can't seem to avoid the conventions of language, and what we write is so very conventional. Of course, I have students who don't know the rules, but nobody ever stands up to denounce goody-goody students who follow the rules right over the cliff, taking their writing with them.

• • •

My wife cannot seem to understand that when I dictate to her at the typewriter I am trying to hear a voice within my skull that she cannot hear and that I can barely hear. There's nothing on paper, yet, nothing in memory, yet, just a hint of a voice which may speak and may say something which may not disappear under my own editorial pen.

Listening for that voice I do not want to hear her voice, or any voice. I must concentrate when there is an interruption and hold myself intensely empty so that the voice can, that voice that is not yet heard, stay where it is in the dark cave until the interruption is over and I can listen for it.

I fear that I ask my students too many questions, suggest too much, praise too much, make educational noise, and get in the way of their hearing what they have to say.

• • •

As I write I often feel the piece of writing forming itself. My students do not need to study form to know form. Form is not made, then poured full of information. Form, like a clay pot, rises from information under the pen.

• • •

In each piece of writing I see at least one technical problem to be solved. In a way, a piece of writing could be defined as an answer to a problem of craft. Can I write this in the first place? Can I dramatize this kind of theoretical piece? Can I tell this essay from the inside, from the writer's point of view?

The reader does not need to know these problems. In fact, I often have to help my students take down the scaffolding of problems they had to solve to make the piece of writing.

One reason that research into the writing process which moves backward from product to process often seems ridiculous to the writer, is that the reader cannot assume from the final published draft what the problems were which are answered by it.

• • •

My writing, at least, does not come from unusual words, but the explosion of meaning which comes from the unexpected collision of ordinary words. When I watch my writing I often see a miniature fireworks display, as words and phrases collide, explode, and ignite further explosions on the page.

• • •

Sometimes in the quiet of my desk I can feel my brain working, chugging away, thinking up problems, and then laboring at them, an intellectual engine hard at work. But most of the time I write not by a matter of accumulation, the linear lining up of facts, the way so many of my students have to unlearn to write.

When it goes well for me, writing is often like looking at a blank screen and then seeing the pattern of an intellectual problem and solution appear at the same time. A click. Another problem and another solution. Click. Another. Click. Another. Lines and shapes, arrows, circles, triangles, lists, boxes, lines, rectangles. Some of these appear on my notebook page, more are just in my head. Many do not have words connected with them, but they are writing.

• • •

I used to be on newspaper rewrite, and I respond to deadlines the way a punchdrunk fighter staggers from an imaginary corner when he hears a bell. And yet I've learned not to force the writings. I have to keep the writing muscles exercised and the motto, "nulla dies sine linea"—never a day without a line—hangs over my writing desk. I start the day by turning on a timer and writing for fifteen minutes; I discipline myself to get to the writing desk and hope for two hours a day, five days a week. And if I am not at the writing desk, I am never far from my canvas office which is filled with pen refills, ink, notebook, clipboard, staples, scissors, paperclips—anything I might need to capture writing if it comes. But waiting for writing to be captured I have to make myself relax. The more at rest I am at my writing desk, the less busy I am, the more productive I become.

• • •

Often I have to write badly to write well. My students want to write too well, too early. I have to get them to put something down on the page, no matter how bad it is, so they can see and hear what they have to work with.

There's something marvelously satisfying with finishing a draft, no matter how bad it is. Now I can go to work. Before the piece of writing was all idea and vision, hope and possibility, a mist. Now it is ink on paper, and I can work it.

• • •

It's wonderful fun to invade a piece of student writing. The better the writing is the more tempted I am to get inside it, to manipulate it, to make it mine. And sometimes in conference I will tell a student, "This is a really good piece of writing. Do you mind if I mess with it?"

She looks apprehensive but she is a student. She nods okay.

Gleefully, I mess around for a few lines or a few paragraphs. I sharpen, I cut, I develop; I add my words for hers, my rhythm, my meaning.

"That isn't right at all. That doesn't sound like me," she says. "That isn't the way it was. Give me back my writing."

She grabs it from my desk and charges out of the office.

Good. She has the feel of writing.

One way to share my own feelings about my own problems in writing is to give my students copies of something I have called "One Writer's Canon" over the years. There are a number of these floating around, for they're a sort of New Year's resolution list, and sometimes I've made a number in a year. Writing a "Canon" is one of the 3,822 ways I avoid writing. What follows is my most recent version. Several colleagues have thought I should include it in this book, for it's one way a student can be taken into a writer's workshop. This list is, of course, eccentric and personal. It's not a list for anyone else, and it will not be my list six months or a year from now.

8
One Writer's Canon - 1982

Priorities. Establish a priority list and deal with each writing project in sequence. Know what you'll be working on the next morning before you go to bed at night.

nulla dies sine linea. "Never a day without a line," Horace, Pliny, Trollope, Updike. Write the first fifteen minutes every morning. Keep a day book. Make use of fragments of time. Make writing a natural part of each day.

Archibald MacLeish: "The first discipline is the realization that there *is* a discipline—that all art begins and ends with discipline—that any art is first and foremost a craft."

Andre Debus: "Talent is cheap. What matters is discipline."

Robert B. Parker: "There is no one right way. Each of us finds a way that works for him. But there is a wrong way. The wrong way is to finish your writing day with no more words on paper than when you began. Writers write."

Alexander Calder: "If you keep working, inspiration comes."

Simone de Beauvoir: "A day in which I don't write leaves a taste of ashes."

Previously unpublished.

Space. After warming up for the first fifteen minutes, give yourself an envelope of time in which to wait for writing. Shut the door, unplug the phone. Do not read, prepare, file, make charts.

> Catherine Drinker Bowen: "What the writer needs is an empty day ahead. A big round quiet space of empty house to, as it were, tumble about in."
>
> Raymond Chandler: "Two simple rules. A) You don't have to write. B) You can't do anything else. The rest comes of itself."
>
> John Galsworthy: "I sit. I don't intend."
>
> Flannery O'Connor: "Every morning between 9 and 12 I go to my room and sit before a piece of paper. Many times I just sit for three hours with no ideas coming to be. But I know one thing: If an idea does come between 9 and 12, I am there ready for it."

Rehearse. Remember that at least 70% of the writing process takes place before the completed first draft. Find the problems to be solved by this piece of writing and guess at a solution. Do not write until you have a possible title, lead, end, sequence, and until you hear the voice.

> Maxine Kumin: (The writer is) "looking for the informing material."
>
> Virginia Woolf: "As for my next book, I am going to hold myself from writing it till I have it impending in me: grown heavy in my mind like a ripe pear; pendant, gravid, asking to be cut or it will fall."
>
> Joyce Cary: "The work of art as completely realized is the result of a long and complex process of exploration."
>
> Elie Wiesel: "With novels it's the first line that's important. If I have that the novel comes easily. The first line determines the form of the whole novel. The first line sets the tone, the melody. If I hear the tone, the melody, then I have the book."
>
> Paul Horgan: "The most important sentence in a good book is the first one: it will contain the organic seed from which all that follows will grow."
>
> Joan Didion: "What's so hard about that first sentence is that you're stuck with it. Everything else is going to flow out of that sentence. And by the time you've laid down the first *two* sentences, your options are all gone."
>
> John McPhee: "I want to get the structural problems out of the way first, so I can get to what matters more."
>
> William Gibson: "I always know the end. The end of everything I write is somehow implicit from the beginning. What I don't know is the middle. I don't know how I'm going to get there."

Katherine Anne Porter: "If I didn't know the ending of a story, I wouldn't begin. I always write my last line, my last paragraphs, my last page first."

Eudora Welty: "I think the end is implicit in the beginning. It must be. If that isn't there in the beginning, you don't know what you're working toward. You should have a sense of a story's shape and form and its destination, all of which is like a flower inside a seed."

Denise Levertov: "You can smell the poem before you can see it. Like some animal."

Write fast. When the writing comes, write fast. Dictate if possible. Let language lead you to meaning. Finish a draft so it can be rewritten, revised or edited.

Walker Percy: "It's a matter of letting go. You have to work hard, you have to punch a clock, you have to put in your time. But somehow there's a trick of letting go to let the best writing take place.

John Fowles: "Follow the accident, fear the fixed plan—that is the rule."

Jayne Anne Phillips: "It's like being led by a whisper."

Edward Albee: "I write to find out what I'm thinking about."

E. M. Forster: "Think before you speak, is criticism's motto; speak before you think is creation's."

John Updike: "Writing and rewriting are a constant search for what one is saying."

Stop in mid-sentence on a long product. Never end on the last line of a chapter, section or scene; with a completed paragraph or sentence. Stop where you can pick up the line and finish it the next day.

Quit if the writing doesn't come. Good writing can't be forced. You'll write again. The writing should flow easily. The writing doesn't come easily when you are writing too soon, taking yourself too seriously, or establishing unrealistic standards.

William Stafford: ". . . one should lower his standards until there is no felt threshhold to go over in writing. It's *easy* to write. You just shouldn't have standards that inhibit you from writing."

Listen. The writing will tell you what needs to be added, cut, or reordered. The final draft should be true to the evolving standards of the text.

William Faulkner: "The material itself dictates how it should be written."

This is one of my favorite pieces, for I think it gets inside the writing act.

9
Listening to Writing

In trying to write an essay which would speculate about how the writer discovers the draft which marks the watershed between prewriting and rewriting, I heard a poem. And in hearing the poem I found this essay which made me newly aware of the importance of listening to writing—both as a writer and a teacher of writing.

A poem was unexpected. As much as I welcome the surprises which are central to the writing process, I felt a bit guilty. Poetry was not on the agenda. I had just finished a draft of a novel and was beginning to revise it. That had first priority. I had this article to do, and it was fighting the novel for first priority as the deadline approached. I had a busy schedule of teaching, traveling, and talking this spring. There was no time for poetry. But on a Saturday, when I had a clear day at home, a day when I had programmed myself to split the morning between editing the novel and drafting this essay, I spent the morning on a poem. When a poem comes, I listen. I have to remind myself that the purpose of my writing routine is to make me receptive to writing—the writing that wants to make its voice heard. That is not always the writing which is expected but I must seize the gift and toss aside the schedule.

It is my habit to begin the day grinding coffee and putting the kettle on the stove. When the pot boils I sit down and twist the dial of a pocket timer to fifteen minutes. I open a 10 by 8 inch narrow-ruled spiral notebook (National 33-008) with green eye-ease paper on my beanbag lap-desk, and uncap my pen (Esprit DLX with black ink and 0.5mm superfine point).

The tools are important. Most craftsmen are compulsive about their tools, and writers work with pen, pencil, typewriter and paper which are familiar to hand and eye. Secretly, I think most writers believe the writing is either in the page or the pen, somehow magically released by the act of writing.

Time is also important. I try to start each day with a few quiet moments when I listen for writing, listen to hear the words I watch my pen put on the page. I may hear—and capture—drafts, titles, lines, leads, details, lists, ideas,

Published in *Composition and Teaching,* December, 1980.

memories, scenes, notes for stories, textbooks, reportage, profiles, essays, poems, plays; whatever comes to my ear is captured on the page. The quiet moments when this happens have a religious quality for me. This quiet time is made possible by habit. I do not get up eager to write. I do not get up even eager to get up. But it is my habit to turn on the timer, open the notebook, uncap the pen, and listen.

Writing usually comes—100 words, 5, 152, 18, 249. No matter. I am simply waiting, listening. If no words arrive at my ear I may think back to a moment of intense feeling—when I was eight and found Grandmother collapsed on the stairs or the moment in combat when I knew I could kill. Or I may brainstorm, catching the specific and apparently unrelated fragments—images, words, details—which pass through our minds as we meditate. I may describe the plant on the table across the room or the scene in the corridor outside the classroom yesterday, because description best ignites writing. I may also play with words. For example, in thinking about my mother's militant Christianity I was interested when I heard two words collide: angry prayers. Those words may give off a poem, a story, an essay, or flicker out and die. It does not matter, at this time, what—if anything—is produced.

If no words come that is fine. I suppress the panic I feel at silence. There will be another day; the writing will come if I wait, and I often do have to wait minutes which seem like hours. My students tell me after they write in class that they had to wait ten minutes, fifteen minutes, half an hour before they could get going. I have timed their long periods of waiting; it seems a long time to them, but it is often only 30 seconds, 105 seconds, 90 seconds, sometimes even 120 seconds. We are educated for busyness, not educated for listening to our own minds at work. I worry more, in fact, when my words come too easily. It is important that I discipline myself to sit down and be quiet, but I am not an assembly line, I do not have to produce. The irony, of course, is that the more peaceful I am, the more quietly receptive, the less I drive myself to produce, the more productive I become.

I try to come to my 15-minute appointment with the blank page as empty of conscious intent as possible. I want no internal noise—the carping of the critic at my last piece, the echoes of past failure or past success, the sandbox bickering of campus politics, the endless listing of what isn't done and must be done—to interfere with what I may hear. External noise does not bother me and I usually write in the morning with the television news or a classical FM music program in the background, but the internal noise of my own busyness can create so much noise I cannot hear my own voice and therefore cannot write.

Of course, I do not really come emptyheaded to any morning's writing. When I am most clear of intention my life lies raw and open to my pen. The other evening, at a poetry reading by Heather McHugh, my notebook was open, my pen uncapped. The better the poetry reading, the more likely that unexpected lines of poetry will arrive. I was ready for the line that rose from within myself: "The dead swim in the earth."

The next morning these four lines slowly arranged themselves on the page:

the father who has buried his daughter
knows the dead swim in the earth
whales shapes of memory rising
to make him stagger as he walks

I have to listen to my autobiography, no matter how painful it is. I must hear the writing which demands to speak.

Every writer—student or professional—comes to the page with a personal history as a human being and as a writer; I am well aware of how my autobiography brought me, on that Sunday morning, to the poem which is central to this essay. I have been a writer since I published a fourth-grade newspaper by hectograph. I have wanted to be a drawer and a painter, and still do. I have long been concerned about the making of art. New poetry usually arrives in bunches, like a car full of uninvited relatives.

Three other forces had impelled me towards a poem. I had made notes on a plane flying home from Charlotte, North Carolina, playing with the idea of a book of poetry called, "An Essay on the Line," which would tell the important things about lines, dots, curves, squares, and triangles my high school geometry book left out. I had had lunch two days before with a fine artist on our faculty, John Hatch, who had talked about how a painting talks to him while he is living within the act of painting. He had given me a marvelous quotation by Cennino Cennini on how the artist discovers "things not seen, hiding themselves under the shadow of natural objects." The mail brought me word that several poems had been accepted and, like my students, I am motivated more by acceptance than rejection. So, on Sunday morning, I found my pen putting down:

```
AN ESSAY ON THE LINE

THE LINE
THE LINE COMES FROM WHAT THE HAND
DIDN'T KNOW IT KNEW
  LINE
THE  TELLS THE HAND WHAT IT KNEW

THE LINE IS (RECOGNIZED) NAMED
IT IS A HAND
REACHING
```

LINES MAKE CONNECTIONS
OF THEIR OWN
IF THE HAND THAT IS DRAWING THEM
~~SEES~~
FINDS THEM

THIS LINE IS A ROCK
THAT A STONE
IS A TREE
THE LINE CRACKS THE STONE
IT

BUT THE TREE IS NOT THAT TREE
OVER THERE
THE STONE
THE ONE ONCE SEEN

IT IS THE STONE
ON THE PAGE
WITH ITS OWN HISTORY
OF FROST AND WARM
THE INSIDIOUS WATER
THE ICE
THE TREE WHICH HAS BECOME
A PART OF IT

ON THIS PAGE
IT IS NOT A STONE
SPLIT BY A TREE
OR A TREE SPLITTING
A STONE

IT IS A STONE TREE
A TREE STONE

MADE ONE BY THEIR
~~NOT~~:SHAPED HISTORY

(MOVE EARLIER?) THE PAGE FLUTTERS
TO THE GROUND

THIS TREE ROCK
SPLITTING THIS PAGE
IS TOO REAL A TREE
TO BE TRUE

```
THE HAND MOVES A ROCK
WHICH HAS BEEN
SPLIT BY A TREE
A ROCK OF HALVES
~~NOT KNEW~~
NO LONGER KNOWING EACH OTHER

THE HAND
TEARS UP THE PAGE
```

That was fifteen minutes' writing, perhaps a bit more self-conscious than normal because it was a poem about art. I was aware of how didactic the first lines were, but I suppressed the critic and did not worry at this time about how unpoetic most of the other lines were. I have to listen to the writing and nothing else. I have to try and hear the soft but true voice hidden under the loud but clumsy voice in an early draft. I have learned that writing evolving often stumbles, but what seem to be mistakes often turn out to be keys to meaning.

I was surprised and excited when one line made a rock and another line a tree. I had no idea that would happen, but when it did, I had something that was real in my mind's eye. I could study the rock and the tree to see what they meant. I felt then the poem might grow into a piece of writing, not a statement about writing. There was no calculation which produced that rock, that tree; they weren't pre-thought. This is not automatic writing in the sense it is dictated from a spirit world, and it is not an un-intellectual act. It is both intensely intellectual and intensely emotional as language brings thought, feeling, and experience together on the page. I live in a New Hampshire landscape of rocks and trees. I experience rocks and trees, I feel rocks and trees, I think about rocks and trees. I did not, however, consciously remember that landscape, and I could not see it from the chair in which I sat. It is such surprises of sight and insight more than anything else that motivate me to write.

When I wrote, "it is a stone tree/ a tree stone," I felt I was on the track of something—that I heard a true voice—but I didn't know if I had or what it was saying. There need be no conscious thought at this point in the writing process. These words are not recorded as a result of conscious decision as to their worth, there is no censor at this stage of the process, the pen writes and later the mind considers and reconsiders what the words mean.

During the process of revision the mind is more consciously engaged. We will write nothing but garbage if we do not practice criticial thinking towards the end of the writing process, but it is dangerous to be too critical too early. The better educated the writer, the more important it is to suspend the critical element of that education in the early stages of the process. The crimes committed by the writer should, in the beginning, all be unpremeditated. On this early draft I was a dog cocking my ears to a strange and distant sound. Perhaps this sound could be described as a problem to be solved. But I did not rush to attack it. I kept drifting along, my ears cocked, allowing words to appear on my page, seeing the energizing relationships the arrows indicate. Then the timer pinged and I capped the pen, closed the notebook.

After breakfast I went downstairs to my desk, again expecting to work on the novel. But the poem spoke first and I had to turn to the typewriter to see how it would look on the page.

The Line
(for John Hatch)

the line comes from what the hand
didn't know it knew

~~the line tells the hand~~
~~what it knew~~

~~this line is a rock~~

this line becomes a rock
that line a tree that cracks the stone

but the tree is not that tree
over there
the rock
not ~~the one~~ once seen at Pemaquid

it is the rock on the page
with its own history of frost
ice water earth see tree

this tree
splitting this granite rock
is too real a tree
to be true

the paper flutters to the ground

the hand
makes a rock split by a tree
a rock of halves
no longer remembering each other

the hand tears the paper
from the board

```
                the line leads the hand
                across the page

                it is not a stone
                split by a tree
                or a tree splitting
                stone

                the line shows the hand
                a stone tree
                a tree stone
not parts but whole <-

         that -> a face hidden from the eye
                is shown by the line hand
                led by the line
```

The visual aspect of discovering writing is important but in doing the research for this article I discovered hearing was more important than seeing, at least in creating the draft which marks the dividing line between prewriting and rewriting. I had thought writing appeared on the page, surprising my eye. I intended to describe and probe that process in this article. But in using myself as my own experimental rat, I discovered I heard the writing in my head an instant before it appeared on the page. I was talking to myself when I was writing, listening to what I had to say.

As I realized the importance of this sequence of listening and then seeing, I began to understand why I usually write the first drafts of poems by hand; then, when they seem ready to be tested—to stand by themselves—I type them. It is, I suppose, the first stage in the process of detachment which must take place if a piece of writing is going to move towards its own identity.

The process seems visual, but the words are first heard in my head and the line breaks are first heard, then typed. The lines may change as I read and edit, trying to help the poem arrange itself on the page, but the final test is how the lines sound rather than how they look.

When I started the article I had a subtitle—how language leads to meaning but that doesn't seem to be the process I follow. As my colleague, Professor Thomas Carnicelli, pointed out, my process doesn't seem to be so much linguistic as imagistic, a process of seeing, then recording in language. Rebecca Rule, a writer, added that as the image is written down it is heard more clearly. In this poem I said in those first didactic lines what I intended to explore, then I heard and wrote so I could see what I had heard. As I examine what I usually do as I write, I feel there is a constant productive tension between what is seen and what is said.

Sometimes I fear my literary colleagues, whose business, after all, is criticial thinking, want to know what criteria are used in accepting or rejecting a discovered thought as if the criteria were external to the piece of writing.

When writers, rather than critics, talk of their own writing to each other and to themselves, they ask what works and what doesn't work. In a real sense they ask the writing what works and listen by reading—often aloud—to the piece of writing's answer. The writer avoids external critical standards—standards which evolved from other pieces of writing in other times by other writers for other readers—and works within the piece of writing. The writer listens to the evolving drafts, "talking with the work" in John Hatch's phrase, to discover its own demands.

Some of what the writer does as he or she reads and rereads, listening to the evolving drafts (and we need careful study of just how but writers read drafts), may involve some of the following considerations:

- What information, symbolized by language, is telling us what meaning will evolve? What information clarifies or confirms that evolving meaning?
- What form, order, structure is evolving? What discipline—limits, focus—is the draft imposing on itself?
- What additional information is being attracted to the draft? What more does the writer—and eventually the reader—want to hear from the piece of writing? What questions have to be answered by the piece of writing?
- What does the voice of the draft tell the writer about the writer's point of view towards the subject?
- What is true to the draft? What is the truth—the meaning—of this draft?

It is important, however, that the writer keep such considerations lightly in mind while writing and rewriting, not to think of them too consciously or they will make so much noise the writer will not hear what the piece of writing is telling him or her to write. The writer must let the piece of writing take its own course as much as possible.

As I typed this draft, for example, I was aware I would have a problem deciding between stone and rock, and I was tempted to fiddle with it right away. But I let the draft speak and delayed the decison; I felt the poem would tell me the answer as I turned to the typewriter again.

```
~~The Line~~   The Rocktree
                 (for John Hatch)

               ~~the line comes from what the hand~~
               ~~didn't know it knew~~

               this line becomes a rock
               that line a tree that cracks the stone
```

I continued to type what I heard in my head, extending the poem, but I have not reproduced it all here for the most important changes came in the reading as I listened to the poem, pen in hand. I had typed "rocktree" near the end of the poem. "Rocktree" it was, and the title represented the fact. The exposition at the beginning became unnecessary; it could be cut away. The poem said it was strong enough to begin to speak for itself.

Towards the end of that draft I heard the poem more clearly.

the hand pulls back — not parts but whole
from the line — a nation with a common
history of winters

A ~~the~~ rocktree
Once
hidden from the eye
remains

~~it is not seen by the eye~~
~~but the hand which follows~~
~~the line~~

I saw the artist's hand pull back and that action had to be reported. The pulling back proved to be significant, for the drawing of the rocktree within the poem and the poem itself were detaching themselves from their maker. The flawed and incomplete endings were necessary. They had allowed me to hear the poem in the beginning, but now the scaffolding could begin to be removed. Elizabeth Bowen talks of "what is left after the whittling away of alternatives." Listening to a draft means, in part, paying attention to what belongs, what drives it towards its own meaning.

In the next typing, the poem pulled itself together a bit more, and my ear, listening to the poem, worked out the problem of stone and rock. It was typed again—the fifth draft—and then the Cennini quotation was added in the sixth draft. There were no changes in that final typing, but I could not know that until I typed it and listened to the poem.

"this is an occupation known as painting,
which calls for imagination, and skill of hand,
in order to discover things not seen, hiding
themselves under the shadow of natural objects,
and to fix them with the hand, presenting
to plain sight what does not actually exist."

Cennino Cennini c 1370

The Rocktree
(for John Hatch and Cennino Cennini)

this line becomes a rock
that line a tree that cracks the rock

but the tree is not that tree
over there
not the rock
once seen at Pemaquid

it is a rock
growing out of paper
with its own history of frost
ice water earth seed tree

still
this tree
splitting this granite ledge
is too real a tree
to be true

the paper flutters
to the ground

the hand makes another rock
split by a tree
a rock of halves
no longer remembering each other

the hand tears the paper
from the board

the hand allows the line
to lead the hand

it is not a rock cut by a tree
not a tree that can slice stone

the line shows the hand
not parts but whole
a nation with a common history
of winters

the hand pulls back
from the line

a rocktree
once hidden from the eye
remains

Donald M. Murray

"Rocktree" tells me something I had learned as a writer but did not know until this poem told it to me: the central act of writing is listening.

The experience of the poem also reminded me that I must somehow, as a teacher, a husband, a son, a father, a friend, a colleague, a citizen, a professional, a busy-busy-busy man so proud of my busyness, find time to listen so I will hear what I have to say. If I am able to be quiet within myself something may appear on the page which may become writing and, when that happens, my job is to listen to the evolving writing. The piece of writing will, if I listen carefully, tell me how it needs to be written. It will develop its own shape and form, its own destination, its own voice, its own meaning, and it will finally detach itself from its maker and find readers who may hear things in it I never heard.

It is important we make the student listen to each draft to hear what has to be done—and not done—next. Our normal educational pattern is to tell the students to look to textbooks or to remember lectures although what has been said often bears no relationship to the work at hand and may, in fact, cause the student to tune out what the draft is saying and therefore ruin it. We also counsel students to pay most attention to what they learned from previous writing tasks but each piece of writing has its own history, and each new piece must be listened to as if the writer were writing for the first time.

It may be helpful, however, to articulate some of the questions which published writers no longer need to articulate while they are listening and relistening, writing and rewriting. These questions may help the student to listen to the student's own devleoping work. Such questions include:

- What did you hear in the draft which surprised you?
- What did you hear that was most interesting?
- What sounds best?
- What sounds so right it can be developed further?
- What is the draft telling you?
- What does the draft ask you to include in it?
- What questions does the draft ask?
- What is the draft trying to say?
- What does the sound of the draft mean?
- In what direction is the order of the information in the draft taking it?
- What is the draft telling you about the subject that you didn't know before?

Too often we tell students to listen to what we have to say when students should listen to their own drafts. These questions can be asked by six-year-old beginning writers and hairy-chinned remedial writers. Neither published writers nor beginning students have much control over what a piece of writing says as it is talking its way towards meaning. Both must listen to the piece of writing to hear where it is going with the same anticipation and excitement we feel when a master storyteller spins out a tale.

In writing this, I realize that listening to a piece of writing is similar to listening to a student in conference, class and workshop. In the beginning, neither the piece of writing nor the student knows what it wants to say. If I listen well and perhaps ask a few questions of the writing I may hear what the writing says in the same way that students in the writing conference or workshop hear what they say when they are given the opportunity to speak of their writing and the process which is producing it. We teach more by listening than by lecturing and we write better if we follow Janwillem van de Wetering's advice to "just write easily, quickly" and listen to what the writing is saying.

This process of listening is more dramatic and easily apparent in poetry than in narrative or in non-fiction, but the process seems more similar in all the forms of writing than it is different—at least the way I write.

When I draft a novel, the making of the draft goes on for months. I stop in the middle of a sentence whenever possible and try to put down three pages of draft a morning, listening to the unfolding story as I hear the words in my head describe the sequence of action and reaction. The process of hearing a novel is the same as hearing a poem.

I also go through a similar process in writing an article such as this. I may do more conscious research and structured thinking in preparation for the writing of non-fiction; I may be aware of a predetermined length or form, a specific audience, an external purpose in writing. Still, I have to listen to the writing as it evolves within those limitations—and if I have a strong piece of writing it may bend those limitations a bit, as it did in the case when I had enough quiet time so that when I thought I was writing a traditional educational article I found I was writing a poem and wrapping an article around it.

Teaching writing is often as unexpected. I must listen and the students must do the talking. That does not mean that I am passive, for the act of listening requires immense concentration and patient receptivity. I must create a climate in the writing conference in which students can hear what they have to say so they can learn to listen to their own writing.

Too often, when we teach writing, we give our students the misconception we plan writing, that we intend what will appear on the page. They are frustrated when they are not able to visualize before the first draft what will appear on their page. The students think they are dumb. We must be honest and let them know how much writing is unconscious or accidental. You do not think writing; you write writing.

Of course, even as I say that, I can think of exceptions. The creative process is never too clear, thank goodness. The elements of intention and planning vary depending on our experience, our purpose, our audience, our writing tasks, but the best writing is often unintended. We usually do not know what we want to say before we say it in non-fiction as well as poetry. We should push ourselves—and our students—to write what they do not expect to say, for the excitement of writing is the surprise of hearing what you did not expect to hear.

I did not expect a rocktree. While dictating the first draft of this article I did not expect to hear my voice developing the relationship between listening to writing and listening to students. But I did hear it, and I recognized its significance. It tied together some things I have learned about writing and about teaching.

I resolve to let my students know why I find it necessary to write quietly for at least fifteen minutes early in the morning. There are 96 quarter-hours in a day, and I need to find at least one quarter hour which I can insulate from busyness so I can listen to myself. If I do that, perhaps I will find a few other quarter hours to listen to the work as it detaches itself from me and tells me what it wishes to become. We write well, not by forcing words on the page, but by listening to those words which collect themselves into a meaning while they are recorded on the page by a good listener.

If our students are to become effective writers, then it is our job to help them find at least a few small slices of quiet time—perhaps in class—and show them how to use that time to listen not to us, but to themselves to hear the writing they did not expect to hear.

I would prefer it if the standards of good writing and the elements of a good subject arose from the evolving text within the class. A good subject is one that interests first the writer, and then the reader. Good writing is what makes the reader feel or think, and the best writing is what makes the reader feel *and* think.

Too many teachers, however, feel that there should be external standards for writing. They don't have faith in themselves as readers or faith in their students as readers. This is the way they have been taught: an anonymous authority establishes the standards. I'm reprinting the following handout because colleagues have said that it helped teachers make the transition from the anonymous authority to the authority of the evolving text within the class.

10
The Qualities of Good Writing

1. ***Meaning***
   There must be content in an effective piece of writing. It must add up to something. This is the most important element in good writing, but although it must be listed first it is often discovered last through the process of writing.
2. ***Authority***
   Good writing is filled with specific, accurate, honest information. The reader is persuaded through authoritative information that the writer knows the subject.
3. ***Voice***
   Good writing is marked by an individual voice. The writer's voice may be the most significant element in distinguishing memorable writing from good writing.
4. ***Development***
   The writer satisfies the reader's hunger for information. The beginning writer almost always overestimates the reader's hunger for language and underestimates the reader's hunger for information.

Published in *English Journal,* March, 1979.

5. ***Design***

A good piece of writing is elegant in the mathematical sense. It has form, structure, order, focus, coherence. It gives the reader a sense of completeness.

6. ***Clarity***

Good writing is marked by a simplicity which is appropriate to the subject. The writer has searched for and found the right word, the effective verb, the clarifying phrase. The writer has removed writer so that the reader sees through the writer's style to the subject, which is clarified and simplified.

It is my belief that these qualities are the same for poetry and fiction as well as non-fiction.

The next piece is the article of mine that has been most reprinted. I hope it has helped students—and teachers—see that revision is much more than proofreading.

11
The Maker's Eye
Revising Your Own Manuscripts

When students complete a first draft, they consider the job of writing done—and their teachers too often agree. When professional writers complete a first draft, they usually feel that they are at the start of the writing process. When a draft is completed, the job of writing can begin.

That difference in attitude is the difference between amateur and professional, inexperience and experience, journeyman and craftsman. Peter F. Drucker, the prolific business writer, calls his first draft "the zero draft"—after that he can start counting. Most writers share the feeling that the first draft, and all of those which follow, are opportunities to discover what they have to say and how best they can say it.

To produce a progression of drafts, each of which says more and says it more clearly, the writer has to develop a special kind of reading skill. In school we are taught to decode what appears on the page as finished writing. Writers, however, face a different category of possibility and resposibility when they read their own drafts. To them the words on the page are never finished. Each can be changed and rearranged, can set off a chain reaction of confusion or clarified meaning. This is a different kind of reading which is possibly more difficult and certainly more exciting.

Writers must learn to be their own best enemy. They must accept the criticism of others and be suspicious of it; they must accept the praise of others and be even more suspicious of it. Writers cannot depend on others. They must detach themselves from their own pages so that they can apply both their caring and their craft to their own work.

Such detachment is not easy. Science fiction writer Ray Bradbury supposedly puts each manuscript away for a year to the day and then rereads it as a stranger. Not many writers have the discipline or the time to do this. We

Published in *Subject and Strategy—A Rhetoric Reader,* edited by Paul Eschholz and Alfred Rosa, St. Martin's Press, 1978, 1981. (This was first published in a different form in *The Writer,* October, 1973.)

must read when our judgment may be at its worst, when we are close to the euphoric moment of creation.

Then the writer, counsels novelist Nancy Hale, "should be critical of everything that seems to him most delightful in his style. He should excise what he most admires, because he wouldn't thus admire it if he weren't . . . in a sense protecting it from criticism." John Ciardi, the poet, adds, "The last act of the writing must be to become one's own reader. It is, I suppose, a schizophrenic process, to begin passionately and to end critically, to begin hot and to end cold; and, more important, to be passion-hot and critic-cold at the same time."

Most people think that the principal problem is that writers are too proud of what they have written. Actually, a greater problem for most professional writers is one shared by the majority of students. They are overly critical, think everything is dreadful, tear up page after page, never complete a draft, see the task as hopeless.

The writer must learn to read critically but constructively, to cut what is bad, to reveal what is good. Eleanor Estes, the children's book author, explains: "The writer must survey his work critically, coolly, as though he were a stranger to it. He must be willing to prune, expertly and hard-heartedly. At the end of each revision, a manuscript may look . . . worked over, torn apart, pinned together, added to, deleted from, words changed and words changed back. Yet the book must maintain its original freshness and spontaneity."

Most readers underestimate the amount of rewriting it usually takes to produce spontaneous reading. This is a great disadvantage to the student writer, who sees only a finished product and never watches the craftsman who takes the necessary step back, studies the work carefully, returns to the task, steps back, returns, steps back, again and again. Anthony Burgess, one of the most prolific writers in the English-speaking world, admits, "I might revise a page twenty times." Roald Dahl, the popular children's writer, states, "By the time I'm nearing the end of a story, the first part will have been reread and altered and corrected at least 150 times. . . . Good writing is essentially rewriting. I am positive of this."

Rewriting isn't virtuous. It isn't something that ought to be done. It is simply something that most writers find they have to do to discover what they have to say and how to say it. It is a condition of the writer's life.

There are, however, a few writers who do little formal rewriting, primarily because they have the capacity and experience to create and review a large number of invisible drafts in their minds before they approach the page. And some writers slowly produce finished pages, performing all the tasks of revision simultaneously, page by page, rather than draft by draft. But it is still possible to see the sequence followed by most writers most of the time in rereading their own work.

Most writers scan their drafts first, reading as quickly as possible to catch the larger problems of subject and form, then move in closer and closer as they read and write, reread and rewrite.

The first thing writers look for in their drafts is *information.* They know that a good piece of writing is built from specific, accurate, and interesting information. The writer must have an abundance of information from which to construct a readable piece of writing.

Next writers look for *meaning* in the information. The specifics must build to a pattern of significance. Each piece of specific information must carry the reader toward meaning.

Writers reading their own drafts are aware of *audience.* They put themselves in the reader's situation and make sure that they deliver information which a reader wants to know or needs to know in a manner which is easily digested. Writers try to be sure that they anticipate and answer the questions a critical reader will ask when reading the piece of writing.

Writers make sure that the *form* is appropriate to the subject and the audience. Form, or genre, is the vehicle which carries meaning to the reader, but form cannot be selected until the writer has adequate information to discover its significance and an audience which needs or wants that meaning.

Once writers are sure the form is appropriate, they must then look at the *structure,* the order of what they have written. Good writing is built on a solid framework of logic, argument, narrative, or motivation which runs through the entire piece of writing and holds it together. This is the time when many writers find it most effective to outline as a way of visualizing the hidden spine on which the piece of writing is supported.

The element on which writers may spend a majority of their time is *development.* Each section of a piece of writing must be adequately developed. It must give readers enough information so that they are satisfied. How much information is enough? That's as difficult as asking how much garlic belongs in a salad. It must be done to taste, but most beginning writers underdevelop, underestimating the reader's hunger for information.

As writers solve development problems, they often have to consider questions of *dimension.* There must be a pleasing and effective proportion among all the parts of the piece of writing. There is a continual process of subtracting and adding to keep the piece of writing in balance.

Finally, writers have to listen to their own voices. *Voice* is the force which drives a piece of writing forward. It is an expression of the writer's authority and concern. It is what is between the words on the page, what glues the piece of writing together. A good piece of writing is always marked by a consistent, individual voice.

As writers read and reread, write and rewrite, they move closer and closer to the page until they are doing line-by-line editing. Writers read their own pages with infinite care. Each sentence, each line, each clause, each phrase, each word, each mark of punctuation, each section of white space between the type has to contribute to the clarification of meaning.

Slowly the writer moves from word to word, looking through language to see the subject. As a word is changed, cut, or added, as a construction is rearranged, all the words used before that moment and all those that follow that moment must be considered and reconsidered.

Writers often read aloud at this stage of the editing process muttering or whispering to themselves, calling on the ear's experience with language. Does this sound right—or that? Writers edit, shifting back and forth from eye to page to ear to page. I find I must do this careful editing in short runs, no more than fifteen or twenty minutes at a stretch, or I become too kind with myself. I begin to see what I hope is on the page, not what actually is on the page.

This sounds tedious if you haven't done it, but actually it is fun. Making something right is immensely satisfying, for writers begin to learn what they are writing about by writing. Language leads them to meaning, and there is the joy of discovery, of understanding, of making meaning clear as the writer employs the technical skills of language.

Words have double meanings, even triple and quadruple meanings. Each word has its own potential for connotation and denotation. And when writers rub one word against the other, they are often rewarded with a sudden insight, an unexpected clarification.

The maker's eye moves back and forth from word to phrase to sentence to paragraph to sentence to phrase to word. The maker's eye sees the need for variety and balance, for a firmer structure, for a more appropriate form. It peers into the interior of the paragraph, looking for coherence, unity, and emphasis, which make meaning clear.

I learned something about this process when my first bifocals were prescribed. I had ordered a larger section of the reading portion of the glass because of my work, but even so, I could not contain my eyes within this new limit of vision. And I still find myself taking off my glasses and bending my nose towards the page, for my eyes unconsciously flick back and forth across the page, back to another page, forward to still another, as I try to see each evolving line in relation to every other line.

When does this process end? Most writers agree with the great Russian writer Tolstoy, who said, "I scarcely ever reread my published writing. If by chance I come across a page, it always strikes me: all this must be rewritten; this is how I should have written it."

The maker's eye is never satisfied, for each word has the potential to ignite new meaning. This article has been twice written all the way through the writing process, and it was published four years ago. Now it is to be republished in a book. The editors made a few small suggestions, and then I read it with my maker's eye. Now it has been re-edited, revised, re-read, re-re-edited, for each piece of writing to the writer is full of potential and alternatives.

A piece of writing is never finished. It is delivered to a deadline, torn out of the typewriter on demand, sent off with a sense of accomplishment and shame and pride and frustation. If only there were a couple more days, time for just another run at it, perhaps then...

In the following article I tried to make clear that much of revision is a re-seeing. Revision, for me, is really prewriting; a new vision of the text arises from the process of clarification. It is far more radical a process than many non-writers understand. I hope this article makes some of that process clear.

12
Internal Revision
A Process of Discovery

Writing is rewriting. Most writers accept rewriting as a condition of their craft; it comes with the territory. It is not, however, seen as a burden but as an opportunity by many writers. Neil Simon points out, "Rewriting is when playwriting really gets to be fun. . . . In baseball you only get three swings and you're out. In rewriting, you get almost as mnay swings as you want and you know, sooner or later, you'll hit the ball."

Rewriting is the difference between the dilettante and the artist, the amateur and the professional, the unpublished and the published. William Gass testifies, "I work not by writing but rewriting." Dylan Thomas states, "Almost any poem is fifty to a hundred revisions—and that's after it's well along." Archibald MacLeish talks of "the endless discipline of writing and rewriting and rerewriting." Novelist Theodore Weesner tells his students at the University of New Hampshire his course title is not "Fiction Writing" but "Fiction Rewriting."

And yet rewriting is one of the writing skills least researched, least examined, least understood, and—usually—least taught. The vast majority of students, even those who take writing courses, get away with first-draft copy. They are never introduced to the opportunities of serious revision.

A search of the literature reveals relatively few articles or books on the rewriting process. I have a commonplace book which has grown from one thin journal to 24 3-inch-thick notebooks with more than 8,000 entries divided into prewriting, writing, and rewriting. Yet even with my interest in the process of rewriting—some of my colleagues would say my obsession—only four of those notebooks are labeled rewriting.

Published in *Research on Composing—Points of Departure,* edited by Charles R. Cooper and Lee Odell, National Council of Teachers of English, 1978.

I suspect the term rewriting has, even for many writers, an aura of failure about it. Rewriting is too often taught as punishment, not as an opportunity for discovery or even as an inevitable part of the writing process. Most texts, in fact, confuse rewriting with editing, proofreading, or manuscript preparation. Yet rewriting almost always is the most exciting, satisfying part of the writing process.

The Writing Process

The most accurate definition of writing, I believe, is that it is the process of using language to discover meaning in experience and to communicate it. I believe this process can be described, understood and therefore learned. Prewriting, writing, and rewriting have been generally accepted as the three principal division of the writing process during the past decade. I would like to propose new terms for consideration, terms which may emphasize the essential process of discovery through writing: *prevision, vision,* and *revision.*

Of course, writing will, at times, seem to skip over one part of the writing process and linger on another, and the stages of the process also overlap. The writing process is too experimental and exploratory to be contained in a rigid definition; writers move back and forth through all stages of the writing process as they search for meaning and then attempt to clarify it. It is also true that most writers do not define, describe, or possibly even understand the writing process. There's no reason for them to know what they are doing if they do it well, any more than we need to know grammatical terms if we speak and write clearly. I am convinced, however, that most writers most of the time pass through the following distinct stages.

Prevision. This term encompasses everything that precedes the first draft—receptive experience, such as awareness (conscious and unconscious), observation, remembering; and exploratory experience, such as research, reading, interviewing, and note-taking. Writers practice the prevision skills of selecting, connecting, and evaluating significant bits of information provided by receptive and exploratory experience. Prevision includes, in my opinion, the underestimated skills of title and lead writing, which help the student identify a subject, limit it, develop a point of view towards it, and begin to find the voice to explore the subject.

Vision. In the second stage of the writing process, the first draft—what I call a discovery draft—is completed. This stage takes the shortest time for the writer—in many cases it is written at one sitting—but it is the fulcrum of the writing process. Before this first draft, which Peter Drucker calls "the zero draft," everything seems possible. By completing this vision of what may be said, the writer stakes out a territory to explore.

Revision. This is what the writer does after a draft is completed to understand and communicate what has begun to appear on the page. The writer reads to see what has been suggested, then confirms, alters, or develops it, usually through many drafts. Eventually a meaning is developed which can be communicated to a reader.

The Importance of Discovery

My main concern in this chapter is revision. But to be able to understand what I consider the most important task in the revision process, we have to appreciate the fact that writers much of the time don't know what they are going to write or even possibly what they have written. Writers use language as a tool of exploration to see beyond what they know. Most texts and most of our research literature have not accepted this concept or dealt with its implications.

Elie Wiesel says, "I write in order to understand as much as to be understood." The poet Tony Connor gives a recipe for writing a poem: "Invent a jungle and then explore it." William Stafford states, "You don't know what's going to happen. Nobody does." I have included at the end of this chapter forty-seven other quotations from my commonplace book which testify to the essential ignorance writers feel many times about what they are writing.

In teaching writing I often feel that the most significant step is made when a student enters into the writing process and experiences the discovery of meaning through writing. Yet this process of discovery has not been generally explored or understood for a number of reasons. First of all, it has not been experienced by nonwriters or admitted when it is experienced by writers in the less imaginative forms of writing. One professor of philosophy, after reading a text of mine, confessed he had been ashamed of the way he wrote, that he didn't know what to say or how to say it when he sat down to write. He had to write and write and write to find out what he had to say. He was embarrassed and didn't want his colleagues to know how dumb he was. When he read my book he found his activities were legitimate. I suspect such unjustified shame is more prevalent than we like to admit. Another professor told me recently that he makes assignments he could not complete by his own deadline. He explained, "My students are smarter than I am. I have to rewrite and rewrite many drafts." Yet he neither "confesses" this to his students nor allows them the opportunity to perform the writing task essential for them to achieve publication.

Most professors who are aware of the process of rewriting to discover meaning are uncomfortable thinking about it, to say nothing of discussing it in class. Discovery seems the province of the "creative writer," the writer who deals in poetry, fiction, or drama. Such activities are not quite respectable in the academic community, where we too often have a sex manual attitude: it's okay to read about it as long as you don't do it. But I am an academic schizophrenic, a "creative" writer and a "noncreative" writer. As the chairperson of a rather large department, I spend a good deal of my time writing memos to deans and vice provosts. (That's really creative writing.) I also moonlight occasionally as a corporate ghostwriter. I publish texts, novels, poems, and "papers." And in all of these roles I find the process of discovery through language taking place. I do not agree with the educational segregation of functional and imaginative writing, creative and noncreative writing. I know the process of discovery takes place when I write fiction and nonfiction, poetry and memos. To produce letters, reports, novels, essays, reviews, poems, and academic papers that say something, you have to allow language to lead you to meaning.

In drafting this paper I found myself writing, as I attempted to define the writing process, that the writer, after the first draft, is "not dealing with the vision but a fact." The word vision surprised me. It appeared on the page without premeditation. In reading it over I cut the sentence but decided the word was a better term than *writing* to describe the second stage of the writing process and, working from that point, saw the virtue of using the term *revision* for rewriting and then tried on the term *prevision* for size and found it fit, although I can't find it in my dictionary. I'm not sure that this is a discovery of enormous value, but it was fun; and I think this accident of language, this business of using words I didn't know I was going to use, has helped me understand the writing process a little bit better.

I suspect most of us have experienced many similar discoveries, but we feel it a failure: if we had a bit more IQ, we would have known the right word. I find few English teachers are comfortable with the concept of uncalculated discovery. They simply do not believe the testimony of writers when they say they write what they don't know, and this may indeed be an uncomfortable concept if you spend your classroom hours analyzing literature and telling your students exactly why the writer did what he or she did, as if literature resulted from the following of a detailed blueprint. Writing, fortunately for writers, is much more exciting than that. The writer does plan but keeps adapting those plans to what is discovered on the page.

The writer, however, who lives in the academic community—and today most of us do—is surrounded by people who seem to know precisely what happens in a piece of literature. The other night my colleague, the poet Charles Simic, said his favorite poems were the ones he didn't understand, an unsettling confession in a department of English. It is hard to admit that you don't know what you're doing when you write. It seems a bit undignified, perhaps even cause for the removal of tenure. Surely my governor would think I ought to know what I'm doing when I sit down to write—I'm a full professor, for goodness sake—and yet I don't. And hope I never will.

Listening to a lecture the other day, I found myself doodling with language. (The better the lecture the more likely a piece of writing will start to happen on my notebook page.) From where I sat in the lecture hall, I could see an office door, and I watched a person in that office get up and shut the door against the lecture. It was an ordinary act, yet, for no reason I can recall, I found myself writing this on the page:

> I had an office at a university, an inside office, without window or air. The classrooms up and down the corridor would fill up with words until they spilled over and reached the edge of my half-opened door, a

confident, almost arrogant mumble I could no longer bother to try to understand. Was I to be like the makers of those words, was I already like the students in my own Freshman sections? Perhaps the only good thing about this position was that Mother was dumbly proud and Father puzzled and angry, "Is this where they put you, an educated man? The union would kill me."

If I hadn't killed a man, my life would have seemed trite....

I have followed this short story for only a couple of pages in the past few days. I am ashamed to reveal the lines above—I don't know if they will lead me to a story—but I'm having fun and think I should share this experience, for it is revealing of the writing process. I did not intend to write a short story. I am working on a novel, a book of poems, and articles such as this one. Short fiction is not on the menu. I did not intend to write an academic short story. I do not like the genre. I do not particularly like the character who is appearing on my page, but I am interested in being within his head. I have not yet killed a man, to my knowledge, and I have never been a teaching assistant, although I have known many.

I want to repeat that there was absolutely no intent in what I was doing. The fact that the character had killed a person came as a total surprise to me. It seems too melodramatic, and I don't like this confessional voice, and I do not like the tense, and I have trouble dictating these words from my notebook to my wife, because they keep changing and leading me forward. I do not know if the killing was accidental or premeditated. I don't know the victim. I don't know the method. I don't know if it was imaginary. I do know the phrase "killed a man" appeared on the page. It may have come there because of what the father said; or, since in the next paragraph I discovered that the young man feels this one act gives him a certain distance from life, a sort of scenic overlook from which to view life, perhaps that idea came from the word "position" in the first paragraph. In my lower middle-class background, even a teaching assistant had a position, not a job. A little more of this kind of thing, however, and the story will never be written.

Writers must remain, to some degree, not only ignorant of what they are going to do but what they are doing. Mary Peterson just wrote me about her novel, "I need to write it before I can think about it, write it too fast for thought." Writers have to protect their ignorance, and it is not easy to remain ignorant, particularly in an English department. That may be one reason we have deemphasized the experience of discovery in writing.

Discovery, however, can be a frightening process. The terror of the empty page is real, because you simply do not know what you are going to say before you say it or if indeed you will have anything to say. I observe this process most dramatically at those times when I dictate early drafts of nonfiction to my wife, who types it on the typewriter. We have done this for years, and yet rather regularly she asks me to repeat what I have said or tell her what I am going to say so that she can punctuate. I don't think, after many books and many years, that she really believes me when I claim I can't remember what I've just said or that I don't know what I'm going to say next.

This process is even more frightening when you engage in the forms of writing that take you inside yourself. "There's not any more dangerous occupation in the world," says James Dickey of poetry. "The mortality rate is very, very high. Paul Valéry once said, 'one should never go into the self except armed to the teeth.' That's true. The kind of poets we're talking about—Berryman, Crane, Dylan Thomas—have created something against which they have no immunity and which they can not control."

Finally, many expert readers who teach English, and therefore writing, are ignorant of the process of discovery because it is not, and should not be, apparent in a finished work. After a building is finished, the flimsy scaffolding is taken away. Our profession's normal obsession with product rather than process leads us towards dangerous misconceptions about the writing process. I believe increasingly that the process of discovery, of using language to find out what you are going to say, is a key part of the writing process. In light of this I would like to reexamine the revision process.

The Two Principal Forms of Revision

The more I explore the revision process as a researcher and the more I experience it as a writer, the more convinced I am that there are two principal and quite separate editorial acts involved in revision.

Internal revision. Under this term, I include everything writers do to discover and develop what they have to say, beginning with the reading of a completed first draft. They read to discover where their content, form, language, and voice have led them. They use language, structure, and information to find out what they have to say or hope to say. The audience is one person: the writer.

External revision. This is what writers do to communicate what they have found they have written to another audience. It is editing and proofreading and much more. Writers now pay attention to the conventions of form and language, mechanics, and style. They eye their audience and may choose to appeal to it. They read as an outsider, and it is significant that such terms as *polish* are used by professionals: they dramatize the fact that the writer at this stage in the process may, appropriately, be concerned with exterior appearance.

Most writers spend more time, *much* more time, on internal revision than external revision. Yet most texts emphasize the least part of the process, the mechanical changes involved in the etiquette of writing, the superficial aspects of preparing a manuscript to be read, and pass over the process of internal revision. It's worth noting that it is unlikely intelligent choices in the editing process can be made unless writers thoroughly understand what they have said through internal revision.

Although I believe external revision has not been explored adequately or imaginatively, it has been explored. I shall concentrate on attempting to describe internal revision, suggesting opportunities for research, and indicating some implications for the teaching of writing.

The Process of Internal Revision

After the writer has completed the first draft, the writer moves toward the center of the writing process. E. M. Forster says, "The act of writing inspires me," and Valéry talks of "the inspiration of the writing desk." The writer may be closer to the scientist than to the critic at this point. Each piece of writing is an experiment. Robert Penn Warren says, "All writing that is any good *is* experimental: that is, it's a way of seeing what is possible."

Some pieces of writing come easily, without a great deal of internal revision. The experience is rare for most writers, however, and it usually comes after a lifetime of discipline, or sometimes after a long night of work, as it did when Robert Frost wrote "Stopping by Woods on a Snowy Evening." The important thing to understand is that the work that reads the most easily is often the product of what appears to be drudgery. Theodore Roethke wisely points out that "you will come to know how, by working slowly, to be spontaneous."

I have a relatively short 7-part poem of which there are 185 or more versions written over the past 2 years. I am no Roethke, but I have found it important to share with my students in my seminar on the teaching of writing a bit of the work which will never appear in public. I think they are impressed with how badly I write, with how many false starts and illiterate accidents it took for me to move forward towards some understanding of the climate in a tenement in which I lived as an only child, surrounded by a paralyzed grandmother and two rather childlike parents. The important thing for my students to see is that each word changed, each line crossed out, each space left on the page is an attempt to understand, to remember what I did not know I remembered.

During the process of internal revision, writers are not concerned with correctness in any exterior sense. They read what they have written so that they can deal with the questions of subject, of adequate information, of structure, of form, of language. They move from a revision of the entire piece down to the page, the paragraph, the sentence, the line, the phrase, the word. And then, because each word may give off an explosion of meaning, they move out from the word to the phrase, the line, the sentence, the paragraph, the page, the piece. Writers move in close and then move to visualize the entire piece. Again and again and again. As Donald Hall says, "The attitude to cultivate from the start is that revision is a way of life."

Discovery and Internal Revision

The concept of internal revision is new to me. This essay has given me the impetus to explore this area of the writing process. The further I explore the more tentative my conclusions. This chapter is, indeed, as I believe it was meant to be, a call for research, not a report of research. There are many things

I do not understand as I experience and examine the process of internal revison. But in addition to my normal researches, I am part of a faculty which includes seven publishing writers, as well as many publishing scholars and critics. We share our work in process, and I have the advantage of seeing them discover what they have to say. I also see the work of graduate students in our writing program, many of whom are already publishing. And I watch the writing of students who are undergraduates at the university, in high school, in middle school, and in elementary school. And I think I can perceive four important aspects of discovery in the process of internal revision.

The first involves *content.* I think we forget that writers in all forms, even poetry, especially poetry, write with information. As English professors and linguistic researchers, we may concentrate on stylistic differences, forgetting that the writer engaged in the process of internal revision is looking through the word—or beyond the word or behind the word—for the information the word will symbolize. Sitting at a desk, pausing, staring out the window, the writer does not see some great thesaurus in the sky; the writer sees a character walking or hears a character speaking, sees a pattern of statistics which may lead toward a conclusion. Writers can't write nothing; they must have an abundance of information. During the process of internal revision, they gather new information or return to their inventory of information and draw on it. They discover what they have to say by relating pieces of specific information to other bits of information and use words to symbolize and connect that information.

This naturally leads to the discoveries related to *form and structure.* We all know Archibald MacLeish said that a poem should not mean but be, but what we do not always understand is that the being may be the meaning. Form is meaning, or a kind of meaning. The story that has a beginning, a middle, and an end implies that life has a beginning, a middle, and an end; exposition implies that things can be explained; argument implies the possibility of rational persuasion. As writers bring order to chaos, the order brings the writers toward meaning.

Third, *language* itself leads writer to meaning. During the process of internal revision (what some writers might call eternal revision), they reject words, choose new words, bring words together, switch their order around to discover what they are saying. "I work with language," says Bernard Malamud, "I love the flowers of afterthought."

Finally, I believe there is a fourth area, quite separate from content, form, or language, which is harder to define but may be as important as the other sources of discovery. That is what we call *voice.* I think voice, the way in which writers hear what they have to say, hear their point of view towards the subject, their authority, their distance from the subject, is an extremely significant form of internal revision.

We should realize that there may be fewer discoveries in form and voice as a writer repeats a subject or continues work in a genre which he or she has explored earlier and become proficient with. This lack of discovery—this excessive professionalism or slickness, the absence of discovery—is the greatest fear of mature, successful writers. They may know too much too early in the writing process.

Questions Looking for Questioners

Speculations about the writing process are fun to propose and entertaining to consider, but we will not understand the writing process unless we employ all of the methods and tools of modern research. Hypotheses suggested, such as the existence of an identifiable process of internal revision, must be subjected to tough, skeptical investigation. We must ask uncomfortable, demanding questions of the writing process. We will certainly not get the answers we expect—many of our pet theories will be destroyed—but the answers will bring new and better questions. Research into the writing process will eventually produce an understanding of how people write, which will have a profound effect on our educational procedures. We now attempt to teach a writing process we do not understand; research may allow us to teach what we understand.

The following are some of the questions researchers must ask:

1. How can the process of internal revision be described? The actual process of internal revision should be described in precise terms so we can understand the steps taken by a broad range of professional and student writers as they use language to discover and clarify the meaning of what they are writing. The process should be broken down and analyzed, defined and documented, so we can begin to understand what happens during internal revision.
2. What attitudes do effective writers bring to the task of internal revision? Attitude precedes and predetermines skill. Too often we attempt to teach skills and fail because we have not taught the attitudes which make the skill logical and obvious. It is important to know the attitude of effective revisors (or is it revisionists?) when they come to their own piece of writing. Do they accept the process of revision as a normal part of the writing process, or do they see it as punishment? Do writers expect their understanding of what they are saying to change as they write?
3. How do writers read their own copy? Writers perform a special, significant kind of reading when they read their own writing in process. Writers must achieve a detachment from their work that allows them to see what is on the page, not what they hoped will be on the page. They also must read with an eye to alternatives in content, form, structure, voice, and language. How do they read their own page and visualize the potential choices which may lead to a clarified meaning? How do they listen to the page to hear what is being said and what might be said?
4. What skills does the writer employ during the process of internal revision? There seem to be four distinct areas or types of internal revision. The first involves content, the collection and development of

the raw material, the information with which the writer writes. The next is the form or structure of the writing itself. The last two are the voice and the language employed in the clarification of meaning. It is likely that there are overlapping but identifiable skills employed by the writer in each of these areas. The skills need to be observed and described. One unexplored skill which might help our understanding of internal revision is the writer's use of memory. There seem to be two significant forms of memory employed by the writer: one is the way in which writing unlocks information stored in the brain; the other is the memory of what the writer has previously written within the piece, which influences each choice during the process of internal revision. Another skill might come from the fact some writers say they write with verbs, especially during the process of revision. It might be fruitful to examine how writers use verbs as the fulcrum of meaning.

5. What developmental stages are significant to an understanding of the process of internal revision? Applying our knowledge of how people react to their own world at different ages may help us understand the process of internal revision. There may be significant differences because of sex, levels of intelligence, or social-economic background. Our preconceptions about student willingness to revise may be wrong. Teachers who see rewriting as punishment may believe that students will not rewrite at certain levels of development and may, because of this conviction, discourage rewriting. In fact, their students may wish to revise, to explore the same subject in draft after draft, if they are given the opportunity. There may be a significant relationship between length and revision. Students may want to write longer than their teachers think they can, and the longer pieces students write may have a greater potential for exploration than shorter pieces. There are also indications that considerable familiarity with a subject, experience with a form, and confidence in a voice may increase discovery.
6. What new knowledge may help us understand the process of internal revision? There are significant new discoveries in brain research, for example, which may provide major breakthroughs in how writers write. The most significant article pointing out this new territory is Janet Emig's "The Biology of Writing: Another View of the Process." We also need to apply the latest findings of linguistic studies, rhetorical research, and learning theory to the process of internal revision. We must draw on as many fields as possible to attempt to understand the writing process. What can the teachers of foreign languages teach us? What can we learn from those who are studying the process of creativity in art, in music, in science? What can we learn from those who study the language of mathematics and from those who design and use computers, which employ the language of mathematics to discover meaning in information?
7. What writing tools, habits, environments, or schedules influence the

process of internal revision? Most writers scorn the interviewer's questions about what time of day they write and whether they use pen or typewriter. They feel this is trivia, and it may be, but it also may be significant trivia, for writers among themselves often seem obsessed by such matters. Writers are craftsmen who are greatly concerned with their tools—the texture, weight, size, and tint of paper; the flow of ink and its color; the design of the pen, its feel, and the breadth of its point. Most writers have superstitions about their favorite writing tools, and most of them vary their tools at different stages of the writing process. I write early drafts of poems in longhand (Mont Blanc fountain pen, thin point, permanent black ink, eye-ease green legal ruled paper), but in a stage central to the process of internal revision, I shift to a typewriter so I can see the poem in print. I find that most poets work in this way. Most writers also find certain environments, quiet or noisy, secluded or public, stimulate the writing process. (I hide in a secluded office these days, but I'd work best in a busy restaurant if I could afford to rent a table and if I could be anonymous—an impossibility in a small university town.) Writers usually are compulsive about the hour at which the work seems to go the best. (My present rule is at least 600 words before 9 a.m. every day.) Most writers seem to move towards the extremes of early morning or late at night, when they have the maximum energy or can work best without interruption, or can tap most easily into their subconscious. Writers have rituals or habits—reading or not reading what they have written or stopping in mid-sentence—which stimulate the flow of discovery through writing. These tricks of the trade may be important for students to know, and they may call for different learning styles or curriculum patterns than those normally imposed in school.

8. What subject areas, writing forms, or language patterns stimulate or discourage discovery of meaning through internal revision? We should observe writers at work on the traditionally most creative forms, such as poetry, but also on the less traditionally studied forms, such as technical writing, business letter writing, speech writing, news writing, and so on, to find out how these writers and the forms they use influence the process of discovery of meaning through language. The evidence we have is restricted to very few forms of writing. We need to extend this examination to all forms.
9. How do editors read writing and encourage improvements through the process of internal revision? Editors are highly specialized readers of writing in process who work closely with writers at each stage of the writing process. Yet, as far as I know, there have been no significant studies of how editors read copy, what they discover, and how they communicate with writers. This editing is not proofreading—it is the constructive examination of a draft with directions as to how further drafts may be developed. It should be obvious that editors are highly expert teachers and that they have a great deal to tell us about the writing process and the teaching of that process. They must motivate and employ

techniques of communication which will make criticism constructive, which will stimulate, not discourage, improvement in writing. Their knowledge, attitudes, and skills might be a significant contribution to the understanding of the writing process and the means by which it can be taught.

10. What curricula, teaching environments, and methods encourage the improvement of writing through the process of internal revision? There are increasing numbers of teachers at every level, from preschool through graduate school, who are helping their students learn to write by taking them through the experience of the writing process. We need to observe these teachers at work and see exactly what their students do while they are engaged in the process of internal revision.

Those are just a few of the questions which should be asked of the process of internal revision. Each question will, of course, lead to additional questions. Each answer will produce even more questions, and researchers bringing their own special knowledge to the task will develop new questions. This is an exciting prospect, for the best and most obvious questions about the writing process have, amazingly, not been asked or investigated. We have a frontier ready for exploration.

How We Can Research Such Questions

I can suggest a number of ways to investigate the essential questions of internal revision:

Bring researchers in the writing process closer together with linguists, rhetoricians, and brain or neuroresearchers in teams and seminars to focus their divergent disciplines on an understanding of the writing process.

Examine writers' manuscripts to discover from the evidence on the page how writers read and revise to clarify their meaning for themselves.

Make use of accounts of the writing process—writers' interviews, diaries, journals, letters, autobiographies—to see what writers say they are doing.

Sponsor accounts of writers at work. Encourage writers to keep journals of an evolving piece of work, together with manuscript pages, so that they might become more aware and make others aware of the nature of their concern during the process of internal revision. (Many writers would refuse, of course, but some would not.)

Observe professional writers and editors at work, and interview them to see what they have done. Not many writers will stand still for this, but there may be some who would consent to be observed in a manner similar to the observation of students done by researchers such as Emig (1971) and Donald Graves (1975).

Collect and examine drafts of a number of versions of pieces of writing in many fields, not just examples of "creative writing" but examples of journalism, technical writing, scholarly writing. When I was an editor at *Time,* many copies of every single draft were typed, distributed, and I believe retained. A research project might collect and examine such drafts and perhaps interview the writers/editors who were producing them.

Observe students' writing and follow drafts evolving through the process of internal revision. Perhaps some students, for example, might be willing to read for revision or even revise using a scanner which shows how their eyes follow the text, where they stop and start.

Test the effectiveness of what we find out about the process of internal revision by having our students follow the examples of the writers who read and rewrite to discover what they have to say, and then see if the students' drafts define and refine a meaning more effectively than the early drafts.

These are just a few of the possible methods of researching internal revision. It seems clear, however, that the most productive method of exploring the writing process is the case study. We do not need extensive statistical surveys as much as we need close observation of a few writers and students doing the entire writing process by well-trained observers who follow their observations with intelligent, probing interviews. This method of investigation seems the one which will yield the basic data and concepts which will be tested and developed by other means of investigation.

The Implications for Teaching

If writers don't write what they know, but to learn what they may know, there may be significant implications for teaching, especially in the area of internal revision. Some of them are:

Stupid kids may not be stupid. Students classified as slow may simply have the illusion writers know what they are going to say before they say it. Since they do not know what they are going to write, they may be paralyzed and not write. Such students, once they understand how writers write, may be released from this paralysis. Some slow students may then appear less slow when their writing evolves through towards a subject.

Many articulate, verbal, glib students who are overrewarded for first-draft writing may be released from the prison of praise and high grades and encouraged to write much better than they ever have before.

Unmotivated students may be motivated to write when they find writing an adventure. In my teaching of "remedial" students, the exploration of a subject through many drafts is the single most significant motivating factor. Teachers constantly make the judgment that their least motivated students will not write many drafts, when in fact they are often the students who most quickly write many drafts once they experience the excitement of exploring a subject with language.

An understanding of the process of prevision, vision, and revision may result in the redesign of writing units so that students spend more time on prevision, far less time on vision, and much more time on revision. Students will have a greater opportunity in such units to discover an area they want to explore and more time to explore it.

Research into the writing process may reveal the process of writing to teachers so they will allow their students to experience it.

Finally, an understanding of the writing process may give literature teachers a new appreciation and understanding of the product we call literature. They may be able to read in a way which will help them discover the full implications of what the writer has done and is doing on the page.

Most of these implications could and should be evaluated by educational researchers. The teaching of writing certainly needs far more professional inquiry than the subjective accounts, anecdotes from the trenches, which so many of us, myself included, have produced in the past.

The new interest in the process of writing, rather than the product of writing, opens the door for important and interesting research which can employ all of the tools of the intelligent investigation. It is a job which needs to be done. The process of writing—of using language to discover meaning and communicate it—is a significant human act. The better we understand how people write—how people think—the better we may be able to write and to teach writing.

Appendix: Writers on Prevision, Vision, and Revision

Edward Albee: Writing has got to be an act of discovery. . . . I write to find out what I'm thinking about.

W. H. Auden: Language is the mother, not the handmaiden, of thought; words will tell you things you never thought or felt before.

James Baldwin: You go into a book and you're in the dark, really. You go in with a certain fear and trembling. You know one thing. You know you will not be the same person when this voyage is over. But you don't know what's going to happen to you between getting on the boat and stepping off.

Robert Bolt: Writing a play is thinking, not thinking about thinking.

Truman Capote: If there is no mystery, for the artist, to solve inside of his art, then there's no point in it. . . . for me, every act of art is the act of solving a mystery.

Frank Conroy: Most often I come to an understanding of what I am writing about as I write it (like the lady who doesn't know what she thinks until she says it).

John Dos Passos: Curiosity urges you on—the driving force.

Alan Dugan: When I'm successful, I find the poem will come out saying something that I didn't know, believe, or had intellectually agreed with.

Robert Duncan: If I write what you know, I bore you; if I write what I know, I bore myself; therefore I write what I don't know.

William Faulkner: It begins with a character, usually, and once he stands up on his feet and begins to move, all I do is trot along behind him with a paper and pencil trying to keep up long enough to put down what he says and does.

Gabriel Fielding: Writing to me is a voyage, an odyssey, a discovery, because I'm never certain of precisely what I will find.

E. M. Forster: How do I know what I think until I see what I say?

Robert Frost: For me the initial delight is in the surprise of remembering something I didn't know I knew. . . . I have never started a poem yet whose end I knew. Writing a poem is discovering.

Christopher Fry: My trouble is I'm the sort of writer who only finds out what he's getting at by the time he's got to the end of it.

Rumer Godden: Of course one never knows in draft if it's going to turn out, even with my age and experience.

Joanne Greenberg: Your writing is trying to tell you something. Just lend an ear.

Graham Greene: The novel is an unknown man and I have to find him. . . .

Nancy Hale: Many an author will speak of writing, in his best work, more than he actually knows.

Robert Hayden: As you continue writing and rewriting, you begin to see possibilities you hadn't seen before. Writing a poem is always a process of discovery.

Shirley Hazzard: I think that one is constantly startled by the things that appear before you on the page when you're writing.

George V. Higgins: I have no idea what I'll say when I start a novel. I work fast so I can see how it will come out.

Cecelia Holland: One of the reasons a writer writes, I think, is that his stories reveal so much he never thought he knew.

William Inge: I don't start a novel or a play saying, "I'll write about such and such." I start with an idea and then find out what I'm writing about.

Galway Kinnell: I start off but I don't know where I'm going; I try this avenue and that avenue, that turns out to be a dead end, this is a dead end, and so on. The search takes a long time and I have to back-track often.

Stanley Kunitz: For me the poem is always something to be discovered.

Margaret Laurence: Each novel is a kind of voyage of discovery.

Denise Levertov: Writing poetry is a process of discovery. . . . you can smell the poem before you see it. . . . Like some animal.

C. Day Lewis: First, I do not sit down at my desk to put into verse something that is already clear in my mind. If it were clear in my mind, I should have no incentive or need to write about it. . . . we do not write in order to be understood; we write in order to understand.

Bernard Malamud: A writer has to surprise himself to be worth reading.

William Matthews: The easiest way for me to lose interest is to know too much of what I want to say before I begin.

Mary McCarthy: Every short story, at least for me, is a little act of discovery. A cluster of details presents itself to my scrutiny, like a mystery that I will understand in the course of writing or sometimes not fully until afterward . . . a story that you do not learn something from while you are writing it, that does not illuminate something for you, is dead, finished before you started it.

Arthur Miller: I'm discovering it, making up my own story. I think at the typewriter.

Henry Miller: Writing, like life itself, is a voyage of discovery.

Alberto Moravia: One writes a novel in order to know why one writes it.

Wright Morris: The language leads, and we continue to follow where it leads.

Flannery O'Connor: The only way, I think, to learn to write short stories is to write them, and then try to discover what you have done.

Lawrence Osgood: Writing is like exploring. . . as an explorer makes maps of the country he has explored.

Jules Renard: The impulse of the pen. Left alone, thought goes as it will. As it follows the pen, it loses its freedom. It wants to go one way, the pen another. It is like a blind man led astray by his cane, and what I came to write is no longer what I wished to write.

Adrienne Rich: Poems are like dreams; you put into them what you don't know you know.

Charles Simic: You never know when you begin a poem what it has in store for you.

William Stafford: I don't see writing as a communication of something already discovered, as "truths" already known. Rather, I see writing as a job of experiment. It's like any discovery job; you don't know what's going to happen until you try it.

Mark Strand: What I want to do in a poem is discover what it is that I have to say.

John Updike: Writing and rewriting are a constant search for what one is saying.

Kurt Vonnegut: It's like watching a teletype machine in a newspaper office to see what comes out.

David Wagoner: For me, writing poetry is a series of bewildering discoveries, a search for something that remains largely unknown even when you find it.

Robert Penn Warren: A poem is an exploration not a working out of a theme.

Thomas Williams: A writer keeps surprising himself. . . he doesn't know what he is saying until he sees it on the page.

This article attempts to break down the process of editing into a logical sequence. At the end of the writing process, the means by which the writer gets out of the way and makes the meaning clear is a craft that can be explained in rather explicit detail.

13
Making Meaning Clear
The Logic of Revision

The writer's meaning rarely arrives by room-service, all neatly laid out on the tray. Meaning is usually discovered and clarified as the writer makes hundreds of small decisions, each one igniting a sequence of consideration and reconsideration.

Revision is not just clarifying meaning, it is discovering meaning and clarifying it while it is being discovered. That makes revision a far more complicated process than is usually thought—and a far simpler process at the same time.

It is complicated because the writer can not just go to the rule book. Revision is not a matter of correctness, following the directions in a manual. The writer has to go back again and again and again to consider what the writing means and if the writer can accept, document, and communicate that meaning. In other words, writing is not what the writer does after the thinking is done; writing is thinking.

This also makes revision simpler. There is a logic to the process. The writer needs only a draft, a pen, and a brain. Each editorial act must relate to meaning. That is the primary consideration that rules each editorial decision. Considerations of audience, structure, tone, pace, usage, mechanics, typography are primarily decided on one issue: do they make the meaning clear?

The process of revision—what the reviser does—is fairly simple. The writer cuts, adds, reorders, or starts over. Each of these acts fits into a sequence most of the time. The writer solves the problems of meaning, and those solutions make it possible to solve the problems of order, and those solutions make it possible to solve the problems of voice.

Published in *Journal of Basic Writing,* Fall/Winter, 1981.

Unfortunately, many teachers—and, I have discovered recently, many newspaper editors—do not understand the logic of revision and, therefore, do not encourage or even allow revision. They pounce on first-draft writing and make corrections.

Since most writers have not discovered their meaning in their first draft, the corrections editors make must come from the editors' own preconceptions of what the writing should mean. It comes from the editors' own experience, their own research, their own prejudices. They work in ignorance of the writer's intention and take the writing away from the writer.

When editors or teachers kidnap the first draft, they also remove the responsibility for making meaning from the writer. Writing becomes trivialized, unchallenging, unauthoritative, impersonal, unimportant.

Hemingway told us, "Prose is architecture, not interior decoration..." Premature correction by a teacher or an editor must focus mainly on the decoration, the cosmetics of writing. Of course, writers must spell correctly, must follow the conventions of language that make meaning clear. But the writer must do it in relation to the writer's meaning through the medium of the writer's own voice. Writing is too important to be corrected by the book; it must be corrected in relation to meaning.

When revision is encouraged, not as a punishment but as a natural process in the exploration of the text to discover meaning, then basic writers become motivated to revise. It is a slow but miraculous process. The basic writers spot a hint of meaning that surprises them. Usually the meaning is in a primitive form at the time it is first shared with a teacher or fellow student. Basic writers are urged on. Soon they do not revise to become correct, they revise to discover their individual meaning, to hear their own voices making those meanings clear and to hear the readers' delight as an unexpected meaning is recognized as true.

The making of meaning through revision is a logical craft. Once a student has made meaning, the process can be repeated. It is not an act of magic any more than magic acts are; it is a matter of turning an engine, kneading dough, sewing a dress, building a shelf. The act of revision allows the writer to take something that was not and make it something that is; it allows the writer to achieve the satisfaction of completion, closure.

Revision can be the most satisfying part of teaching composition if the teacher is willing to let go. The composition teacher must wean the student. The teacher must give the responsibility for the text to the writer, making clear again and again that it is the student, not the teacher, who decides what the writing means.

The best way for teachers to reveal exploration in revision is by writing in public on the blackboard, or by using an overhead projector, allowing the students to see how writing struggles to find what it has to say. The teacher should not consciously write badly; the teacher should write as well as possible. That will produce copy that is quite bad enough to deserve revision.

The teacher who writes in public will expose the fact that writing often does not come clear, in fact, syntax often breaks down just at the point where a new or significant meaning is beginning to break out of its shell. That meaning has an awkward and clumsy time of it, but if the writer listens carefully and nurtures the meaning it may grow into significance. Or it may not. It may have to be put aside. But first it has to be understood before it can be rejected. Teachers who are willing to share evolving writing will find their class willing to share in a workshop where everyone is trying to help the writer discover and identify the evolving meaning.

I have internalized a checklist that follows the logic of revision. It may be helpful to consider this checklist, but each teacher should work to develop a new checklist with each class. Neither my checklist nor anyone else's checklist should be taken as gospel. The checklist should be formulated while the class experiences the process of making meaning clear.

The principles that underlies my checklist are:

- *Build on strength.* The writer searches the text for the meaning that is being developed by the writing and looks for what is working to make it work better. Revising is not so much a matter of correction as it is a matter of discovering the strength of the text and extending that strength.
- *Cut what can be cut.* An effective piece of writing has a single dominant meaning, and everything in the text must advance that meaning.
- *Simplicity is best.* This does not mean writing in pidgin English, merely sending a telegram to the reader. It does mean making the writing as simple as it can be for what is being said. The message may be complex, and that may require linguistic or rhetorical complexity, but that complexity should always be the simplest way to communicate the complexity.
- *The writing will tell you how to write.* In revising I do not look to rule books, to models from other writers, to what I have written before, or how I have written it. The answers to the problems of this piece of writing lie in the evolving text. I have faith that if I read carefully—if I listen to my own developing voice—I will discover what I have to say.

My checklist requires at least three different kinds of reading for focus, form and voice. This does not mean that I read the text three times; it is possible that the readings overlap and I read it only a couple of times. Most times I read it many more times. There is no ideal number of readings. I read it enough times to discover what I have to say.

During each of the readings I keep my eye and my ear on the single dominant meaning that is evolving from the text. A good piece of writing, I believe, says only one thing. Or to put it a different way, the many things that are said in a piece of writing all add up to a single meaning.

Here is my internal checklist articulated:

Focus

First, I read the text as fast as possible, trying to keep my pen capped, trying to see it from a distance the way the reader will so I can ask myself the larger questions of content and meaning. I do not do this "first" reading, of course, until I have the meaning of the writing in mind. In other words, I have to have *a* focus before I can work on *the* focus. If, in each stage of the reading, the meaning does not become clearer and clearer, I go back and discover a potential meaning that can be brought into focus. The questions I ask are:

- What does the piece of writing mean? If it isn't clear I will take the time to write a sentence that makes the meaning clear, that achieves what Virginia Woolf calls, "the power of combination," that contains the tensions within the piece of writing in a single statement.
- Are all the reader's questions answered? Many times I will brainstorm the questions that the reader will inevitably ask of the text.
- Is new information needed?
- Is the piece built on undocumented assumptions? Sometimes I will actually write down my assumptions to see if they make sense or stand up as a firm foundation for the piece.
- Is the genre appropriate to the meaning? One of my novels started out as a series of articles. By genre I mean fiction, poetry, or the larger categories of non-fiction—personal narrative, familiar essay, argument, exposition.
- Are there any tangents that can be cut loose? I used to have much more trouble getting rid of those wonderful pieces of evidence or examples of writing that really didn't relate to the meaning. The late Hannah Lees taught me how to solve this problem. For years I wrote one paragraph to a page. Then played solitaire with these paragraphs, analyzed and re-analyzed them until they made a single meaning.
- Is there a section that should be a separate piece of writing?
- Is each point supported by convincing evidence? Sometimes I actually role-play a reader. It is always a specific person I know who does not agree with me and who I believe does not like me. I want to confront my enemies and defeat them before the writing is published.
- Is the piece long enough to satisfy the reader? Most writers underwrite, and I am no exception. The tendency is to say it and not to give the reader enough room to discover the meaning.
- Is the piece short enough to keep the reader involved? The piece of writing must develop its own energy, its own momentum. If my mind wanders during this first quick reading, the reader's certainly will.

Form

Next, I read the text again, a bit more slowly, only uncapping my pen when a marginal note is necessary, trying to look at the text as a sequence of chunks of writing, perhaps chunks of meaning. I am no longer looking at the text as a whole, although I am aware of the territory now, and I am trying to keep myself free of the concern with detail, for a premature involvement with the details of language may keep me from evaluating the questions of form. The questions I ask are:

- Is the title on target? Years ago when I could put my own heads on editorials I found that the effort to write a title is worth the trouble. I may draft as many as a hundred titles, for each one is a way of discovering meaning, and I can draft a number of titles in slivers of time. At this stage of the revision process I check to make sure that the title relates to the meaning as that meaning has now evolved.
- Does the lead catch the reader in three seconds—or less? I hear rumors of good pieces of writing that have poor leads or beginnings, but I have not been able to find any from professional writers. The first few lines of a piece of writing establish the tone, the voice, the direction, the pace, the meaning. I check once more to make sure that the lead will entice the reader.
- Does the lead deliver on its contract with the reader? The lead must be honest. It must relate to the meaning that will evolve through the text.
- Does the piece answer the reader's questions at the point the reader will ask them? This is the key to effective organization. Again and again I will ask questions the reader will ask, even if they are the questions I do not want the reader to ask, and then number them in the order the reader will ask them. A good piece of writing does not need transitional phrases. The information arrives when the reader can use it. The reader's questions and their order can be anticipated.
- How can I get out of the way of the reader and show rather than tell? Orwell instructed writers that they should be like a pane of glass through which the reader sees the subject. I do not want the reader to be impressed with my writing, my arrogance is greater than that; I want the reader to receive the evidence in such a direct fashion that it will cause the reader to think the way I want the reader to think. I want to show so effectively that the reader sees my meaning as inevitable.
- Is there an effective variety of documentation? Most of us fall into a pattern using quotations, citations, anecdotes, statistics, personal experience—whatever we feel comfortable using or whatever we think we do well. The documentation, of course, should be what works best for the point being documented.
- Does the pace reinforce the meaning? The reader should be allowed to absorb each point before moving on to the next one. I tend to write and to teach too intensively; I have to remember to give the reader room.
- Does the pace provide the energy to carry the reader forward?
- Are the dimensions appropriate to the meaning? The size of each section

should be in proportion to other sections—appropriate to the meaning.
- Does the end echo the lead and fulfill its promise?

Voice

At last, I read the text slowly, line by line, my pen uncapped. I usually read the text many times within this category, generally working from the larger issues of voice down to paragraphs to sentences to phrases to single words. This is the most satisfying part of revision. There is a single meaning. It will change and develop and become clearer, but there is a focus, there is an order, and there is the chance to work with language, to combine my voice with the voice that is evolving from the draft. The questions I then ask are:

- Can the piece be read aloud? Does it sound as if one person is talking to one person? Reading is a private experience, a human contact from one single person to another single person. I think that effective writing should be conversational. Sometimes the conversation is more formal than others, but it should never be stuffy, pretentious, or incapable of being read aloud by the writer.
- Are important pieces of specific information at the ends and beginnings of key sentences, paragraphs, sections, and the entire piece itself? The 2-3-1 principle of emphasis can do as much as anything else to sharpen up prose and make meaning clear: the second most important point of emphasis is at the beginning: the least important piece of emphasis is at the middle, and the greatest point of emphasis is at the end.
- Does each paragraph make one point?
- Does each paragraph carry a full load of meaning to the reader?
- Do the paragraphs vary in length in relation to meaning—the shorter the more important the information?
- Are the paragraphs in order? If the reader's questions are answered when they will be asked, formal transitions will not be needed.
- Does the reader leave each sentence with more information than the reader entered it?
- Are there sentences that announce what will be said or sum up what has been said and, therefore, can be cut?
- Are most sentences subject-verb-object sentences? At least most sentences that carry the essence of meaning should be direct sentences. The interesting work done in sentence-combining has too often confused this issue. Of course sentences should be combined, but the strength and vigor of the language still lies in simple, direct subject-verb-object sentences. These are the sentences, short and to the point, that will communicate.
- Are there clauses that get in the way of meaning? Many sentences have to be reordered so that the meaning comes clear. This usually means that sentences have to be read aloud again and again until the information in the sentence appears at the moment that the reader can use it.

- Are the verbs active and strong enough to drive the meaning forward? The verbs are the engines of meaning, and during revision the writer must give priority to finding verbs that are accurate and provide energy.
- Has the right word been found? Many times we try to use two almost right words in the hope that we will trap the meaning between them. That does not work. Mark Twain said, "The difference between the right word and the almost-right word is the difference between lightning and a lightning-bug." He was right. Revision is the search for the exactly right word.
- Does the meaning depend on verbs and nouns, not adverbs and adjectives? The right word is rarely an adjective or an adverb. Again, the meaning is not caught best in the crush between adjective and noun, or adverb and verb. I always feel a tiny sense of failure when I use an adjective or an adverb. I have failed to find the right noun or the right verb.
- Is there sexist or racist language that should be changed?
- Can the writing be more specific?
- Are there unnecessary lys, ings, thats, and woulds that should be cut? Each writer must develop a list of linguistic interferences with meaning. I find when I do professional ghost-editing that merely cutting the lys, the ings, the thats, the woulds—and yes, the unnecessary verb be—will make an obscure text start to come clear.
- Are there unnecessary forms of the verb "to be"?
- Is every fact checked?
- Is each word spelled correctly?
- Is there anything I can do to make the writing simple?
clear?
graceful?
accurate?
fair?

Do I formally ask all of these questions of myself in every piece of writing I do? Of course not. These concerns are internalized, and they overlap. The process is recursive. I discover meaning by language. I work back and forth from meaning to focus to form to voice and from voice to form to focus to meaning.

The process is, however, logical. Everything on the page must reveal meaning. Every word, every space between words, is put on the page or left on the page because it develops the meaning of the piece of writing.

This checklist can not be dumped on the beginning or the remedial writer, but it can be used by the teacher to establish priorities. The student has to learn that writing is a search for meaning, and once a potential meaning is found it may be clarified through the process of revision.

There is a simple guiding logic to revision, and every question of spelling, usage, structure, mechanics, style, content, documentation, voice, pace, development, must be answered in terms of meaning.

Think of a workman who moves in close, measuring, marking, sawing, fitting, standing back to examine the job, moving back in close to plane, chisel, mark and fit, standing back again to study the task, moving in close to nail the piece in place, stepping back for another look, moving in close to set the nails, another step back, another look, then in close to hide the nail holes, to sand, stepping back to make sure the sanding is complete, then in close at last to apply the finish.

Actually the workman probably moved in close many more times before finishing the task and certainly stepped back many times to see the job entire. And so does the writer, working between word and meaning.

What the student can discover is that this process is logical; it can be understood. An effective piece of writing is produced by a craft. It is simply a matter of working back and forth between focus, form, and voice until the meaning is discovered and made clear.

I've used the following handout for many years to show how one writer on one text used a well-sharpened pen to clarify a piece of prose. Most years I've had my students write similar brief descriptions of their writing process, and we share them to show that there is not one way to write, but many ways to write. When I share mine I also show the early edited draft to reveal the editing that often is required for prose to appear spontaneous.

14

HOW I WRITE AN ARTICLE — I THINK

~~AND HOW I FEEL WHILE I'M DOING IT I THINK~~

~~Unless I am completely controlled by a deadline and forced to write before I have completed my research, I am aware that~~ it is time to ~~think about~~ writ~~ing~~*e* when I know the answers ~~I will receive to my questions~~ *to my questions* before I ask them, *when I know what my sources tell me what I already know.*

~~Now~~ I am filled with information, ~~which is not necessarily related to other pieces of information.~~ *and specific details, facts, quotations, phrases rise to the surface of* ~~Fragments of information keep popping into~~ my mind at odd moments *these fragments seem to try and* ~~attempting to~~ connect with other bits of information *as if they were magnetized cells swimming toward and away under the eye of a microscope.* I am intensley aware, and what I see, what I hear, what I read, what I remember, keeps trying to relate to ~~the article I am going to write.~~ *the pieces of information from which my article will be built.*

I ~~may~~ make notes, *in spite of myself, record* fragments of ideas, hints of a voice or a tone, *scribble* a phrase, but ~~mostly~~ I ~~do~~ *try* not *to* concsiously think about the subject. *I try not to think consciously about them, try not to interfere or even observe their mating but* I am simply open to it and I ~~can not keep from thinking about~~ it. When I have a moment of quiet, it rises to the surface of my mind on its own energy. The information ~~I have~~ seems to demand its own order, its own connections, its own structure, and I often find myself *making notes by* drawing designs, or at least lines and arrows, between pieces of information.

¶ ~~Next I usually~~ *almost reluctantly I begin to* write titles— as many as a hundred— at odd moments. Each ~~in its way~~ helps me focus on the subject, limit it, take a point of view towards it, *for every* ~~Each~~ title is a ~~sort of~~ quick draft which ~~at least~~ helps eliminate what doesn't belong. Then I start drafting leads— as many as fifty of ~~them~~ *those—* getting the first line right, the first paragraph right, ~~Occasionally I will go as far as the first~~ *sometimes even* ten lines *right.* ~~But usually it~~

¶ *This* is just the beginning of the beginning, those fiew lines the reader may glance at *in deciding to read or pass on. Those few words, fifty or less establish* ~~It is only a few words and~~ the tone, the point of view, the order, the dimensions of the ~~piece of writing are all established. The~~ *article. An article, perhaps a book, can only say one thing and when the lead is written, the writer knows what belongs and what has to be left out.* ~~choice of a~~ *As one* word *is chosen and another rejected,* a comma *put in and another taken away the* ~~, a dash, the relationship of one word to another word, these matters are all attended to until~~ *lead begins to feel right and* the pressure builds up ~~and~~ *until* it is almost impossible not to go on*, and write.*

Then the entire article is drafted as fast as possible, perhaps with a few fragmentary notes, something far less than an outline. But usually ~~even that is not paid attention to~~. ~~T~~he draft is written without notes. ~~usually~~ *Often* I dictate, ~~speaking without consideration,~~ letting language lead me, allowing the ~~instinctive order of the piece~~ *article* to ~~take~~ shape *itself instinctively*. I am both ~~incredibly~~ intense and relaxed at the same time; ~~E~~verything is concentrated on allowing the article to come out of me on its own energy, ~~in~~ *within* its own *evolving* form.

Now I read it ~~quickly, casually,~~ carelessly, the way a reader will ~~read it~~, to ~~catch the~~ *hear my* voice, to ~~see~~ *spot* the larger holes *in the structure*. Then I reread it ~~perhaps~~ a dozen

My interest span is short. I work in spurts of deep concentration until I become too bored, like too much what I hear myself saying.

times, perhaps more. ~~At~~ first I attend to the larger questions. Do I have a subject? Must I go back ~~to~~ and do more research, ~~to~~ write ~~a~~ new titles, ~~to~~ work further on the lead, ~~to~~ choose a different genre or form? Then I deal with matters ~~such as~~ of order ~~or~~ and structure. I may outline, cut and paste, move chunks of material around. Sometimes I write a paragraph to a page to make this reordering easier. Once the order is firm I look to matters of evidence. Have I documented each point? Then I deal with matters of dimension. Are there parts of the piece of writing which are too long or too short in relationship to each other?

Although I cut ruthlessly, my drafts usually grow longer. I have to develop my points to make them clear to myself and then to my reader.

~~All the time~~ I listen to what I am saying to find out what I have said. I keep making discoveries, larger discoveries at first, then smaller ones. ~~These are discoveries of meaning.~~ I find out what I have to say by saying it. ~~My language leads me towards clarity.~~ ~~Although~~ in the earlier ~~drafts~~ readings I am not so much looking at language as exploring ~~consciously but at~~ the subject, ~~exploring it,~~ trying to see it so clearly I can ~~to~~ understand it. In the later drafts I am looking more ~~consciously~~ at language, trying to get the right word, trying to make the subject clear and ~~myself invisible. Sometimes I feel I am erasing myself so the reader will see the subject, not the writer.~~ what is written, not who is writing.

~~At last I read it so a stranger with absolute detachment, often reading it aloud to hear it as someone will who does not know the subject or even care about it. Then I type it or have it typed so that copy is clean, and the first reader, the editor, will be able to see what I have to say.~~

14
How I Write an Article—I Think

It is time to write when I know the answers to my questions before I ask them, when my sources tell me what I already know. I feel stuffed with information, and specific details, facts, quotations, insights, phrases, relationships rise to the surface of my mind at odd moments. These fragments try to connect with each other as if they were cells swimming towards each other and away under the eye of a microscope. I try not to think consciously about them, try not to interfere with their mating but I am intensely aware, and what I see, what I hear, what I read, what I remember, tries to relate to the pieces of information from which my article will be built.

I may make notes in spite of myself, record fragments of ideas, hints of a voice or a tone, scribble a phrase, but I try not to think consciously about the subject. I am simply open to the subject and when I have a moment of quiet, it rises to the surface of my mind on its own energy. The information seems to demand its own order, its own connections, its own structure and I often find myself making notes by drawing designs, or at least lines and arrows, between pieces of information.

Almost reluctantly I begin to write titles—as many as a hundred—at odd moments. Each helps me focus on the subject, limit it, take a point of view towards it, for each title is a quick draft which helps eliminate what doesn't belong. Then I start drafting leads—sometimes as many as fifty—working to get the first line right, the first paragraph right, sometimes even the first ten lines right. What is right? The start of a clear line through the subject and that something I sense rather than know; following it I will be surprised.

The lead is the beginning of the beginning, those few lines the reader may glance at in deciding to read or pass on. These few words—fifty, forty, thirty, twenty, ten—establish the tone, the point of view, the order, the dimensions of the article. In a sense, the entire article is coiled in the first few words waiting to be released.

An article, perhaps even a book, can only say one thing and when the lead is found, the writer knows what is included in the article and what is left out, what must be left out. As one word is chosen for the lead another rejected, as a comma is put in and another taken away, the lead begins to feel right and the pressure builds up until it is almost impossible not to write.

The article is drafted as fast as possible, always without the research in front of me, occasionally with a few fragmentary notes indicating a rough sequence of ideas, never with anything as formal as an outline. Often I dictate, letting language lead me, allowing the article to shape itself instinctively. I feel both intense and relaxed at the same time; everything is concentrated on

Previously unpublished.

allowing the article to come out of me on its own energy, within its own evolving form.

Now I read the draft carelessly, the way a reader will, to hear my voice, to spot the large holes in the structure of meaning. Then I reread it half a dozen times, a dozen times, perhaps more, worrying it into shape. I have a short interest span and I work in bursts of deep concentration until I become pleased with what I have written. Then I take a break and then return to the attack. But this isn't work, it's fun. I'm making something that has not been made before.

I attend to the larger questions first. Do I have a subject? Must I go back and do more research, write new titles, work further on the lead, choose a different genre or form? Then I deal with matters of order and structure. I may outline now, cut and paste, insert and remove, shift chunks of copy around. Sometimes I write a paragraph a page to make this reordering easier. Once the order is firm I look to matters of evidence. Have I documented each point? Then I deal with matters of dimension. Are there parts of the piece of writing which are too long or too short in relationship to each other? Of course these questions overlap.

Although I cut ruthlessly, my drafts usually grow longer. I have to develop my points to make them clear to myself and then to my reader. I keep being surprised, that's what keeps me going. I find I write what I did not expect to write; my accidents lead me on. I find out what I have to say by saying it.

In the earlier readings, I am not so much looking at language as exploring the subject, trying to see it clearly so I can understand it. In later drafts I look more at language, again trying to make the subject clear. At the end I cut and shape to erase myself so the reader will see what is written, not who is writing.

II

Writing for Teachers

This piece of writing has a peculiar history. Don Miller, now of Oakland University in Michigan, who was then with the Ford Foundation, invited me to write the piece. He felt that much significant educational research was not reaching teachers because of the way it was written. I agreed, and I wrote this piece. We were, of course, naive; we could not get it published in the educational journals where it might have done the most good. In mimeographed form, however, it has had a life of its own, and perhaps it fits here, midpoint between the selections that emphasize the writing process and those that emphasize the teaching process.

I realize that the style advocated is journalistic and not academic. And I realize that that's something that scares many people in our profession. I can, however, point out that most of my articles that have been written in a journalistic style have been published, and that those who have used this article have not only gotten published, they have been read.

15
Write Research to Be Read

The results of educational research might reach classroom teachers, school administrators, schoolboard members, parents, legislators, and taxpayers if researchers would learn from journalists and other non-fiction writers how to write for the general public.

Educational research reports are too often written in a private language and an academic form which obscures their conclusions and excludes those people who might implement the research results.

The craft of clear writing is not a mystery. Writing is a process which can be learned, and the principles of writing for a general audience are clear and simple. They are, in fact, deceptively simple, and that very simplicity is often rejected by the academic mind which confuses complexity with intelligence. Simple writing is easy to describe, hard to perform, yet it can be learned and practiced by persons who have something to say and the courage to communicate.

Previously unpublished; written with support from the Ford Foundation.

The obscurity of research writing may not be critical—although I think this could be debated—in certain of the sciences, where a few members of a private research club write for other members of the same club. But educational research must reach the classroom. Educational researchers must be able to communicate with those who control the classroom if educational research is to have significant impact on our educational system.

There are ten basic principles which should be understood and practiced by the researcher who has the commitment and the courage to write for a general audience. They are:

1. You Can't Write Nothing

The amateur believes a professional writer writes with words, that the pro can erect a solid piece of writing out of rhetoric, grammar, vocabulary and a magic called talent. The writer writes with information. Words are the symbols for information, and if there is no information there will be no effective writing, no matter how graceful or correct the arrangement of the words upon the page. The raw material from which a piece of effective writing can be constructed is knowledge—solid, specific, concrete pieces of information which can be built into a meaning.

The ghostwriter or ghost editor doesn't start with the text but with the subject. The subject is first learned, and the professional must be a quick study. Content precedes form; in fact, content predicts form. Accurate information arranged in a logical and meaningful order will produce writing which will stand up to a reader. As Ernest Hemingway said, "Prose is architecture, not interior decoration."

2. Write to Think

Teachers frequently say, "Know what you want to say before you say it." Writers know that is often false counsel. The professional writes to discover what will appear on the page. Language leads the writer toward meaning. We are all familiar with the process of talking out a problem with another person to find out what we mean and how we feel about it. The writer talks to himself or herself through writing.

Many writers put their notes aside when the time comes to complete a first draft and dictate or write as fast as they can to see what appears on the page. Experience reveals to them that much of what is forgotten needs to be forgotten, and what is remembered is what is important. The subconconscious is a good editor. And, of course, if memory fails, what is forgotten can be recovered from the notes later, for the writer assumes that any piece of writing will evolve through a series of discovery drafts, which first explore and then clarify the subject. The writer knows rewriting is not punishment, but an essential part of the process of using language to discover meaning.

Look at what is happening in these sentences from successive drafts.

- The teachers observed in a succession of schools within this one system seemed both comfortable and competent with the curriculum, which seemed to this observer to repeat much of the Language Arts material year after year.

- The observer thought the curriculum was repetitive, with an excessive overlap from year to year, and it was surprising that there seemed little evidence of boredom on the part of the teachers and their students.
- The observer realized that both teachers and students were comfortable within this curriculum for they were learning little that was new.
- The observer began to realize the resistance to change within the school system when he saw that both teacher and student were comfortable within a traditional curriculum.
- One of the principal reasons for resistance to change was the fact that teachers were teaching what they had taught before to students who had learned it before. Everyone knew what was expected of them. Classrooms had a comfortable feeling. There was efficient performance but little learning.

There are many things going on in those sentences, but the most important thing is that the writer is moving towards meaning, is thinking on the page. The writer works from an observation toward an understanding of its cause. The writer, during the process of writing, is not looking at a handbook, a dictionary, or thesaurus, but is looking through the page at the classroom. The writer is looking at information, symbolizing it with words, and then examining what is on the page to discover what it means. Writing is thinking.

3. Write in Terms of People

The general reader is far more interested in people than in ideas, theories, or concepts. Academics may resent or deplore this, but they must accept it as a condition of work if they want to write for a general audience. Educational researchers, at least, should be comfortable writing about people, for although we need more basic research in learning, in chemical-electric brain functions, still most educational research is, by its nature, research which has direct implications for students and teachers. It should be able to be reported in terms of people.

Writers who achieve a large audience populate their pages with individual persons whose actions reveal the ideas the writer wishes to communicate.

There are two principal techniques of putting people onto a page of writing:

- The basic building block of the popular magazine article is the anecdote, or little story, which reveals a point in terms of people. As an editor once told me, "Your article should be written in parables, the way the Bible is." I laughed, but I learned.

  The researcher might write:

  "The omission of conventional verbalization is often an effective technique of classroom management."

The magazine article writer might write:

"It was a typical after lunch class at Inner City High School. Roscoe gave a peanut-butter belch and Jed, Tom, and Theodore clapped in appreciation. Marianne giggled. Herbert knocked Joan's books on the floor. Hannah flipped a paperclip into Jody's softdrink.

Then Miss Gooch came into Room 212. She was elderly—at least forty years old and four feet eleven inches tall. She wore last year's dress. The observer knew this would be a disaster.

Miss Gooch marched to the exact center of the wall, in front of the obscenity on the blackboard and looked right at Hannah. When she caught her eye she turned to Jody, and then Herbert, and then Theodore, Tom, Jed, Roscoe and, one by one, they grew quiet. The silence grew louder and louder until she said in a soft voice, 'My name is Lucinda Gooch.' No one laughed.

Research has documented what Miss Gooch knew. Silence can be an effective tool in classroom management."

- The other technique is simply to perk up a general statement by populating it with people when it can clarify the meaning.

The researcher might write:

"It is dysfunctional educative practice to postulate on-site, in-service, participatory sessions when school practitioner fatigue has multiplied the tri-administrative managerial inter-face malfunctions."

The writer might say the same thing this way:

"At 2:50 the bell rings and students stampede from the school. They are released for the day, but the teachers aren't. Clutching papercups of instant coffee, juggling armloads of papers to be read that night, muttering threats of a yawn-in, they slump off to an in-service training session."

Obviously a piece can be made too perky, cluttered with people or filled with anecdotes and descriptions that obscure what is being said. But most research in education never lets the reader see what has been studied in terms of the individuals examined and shown what it means to individuals in the classroom. And that is one reason educational research is rarely read and rarely implemented.

4. Say One Thing

An effective piece of writing has focus. There is a controlling vision which orders what is being said. The writer writes drafts to establish the priority of meaning, and then eliminates all that doesn't follow. In this article the dominating idea was that educational researchers could and should learn the principle of writing for a mass audience. When that idea is established, every page, every paragraph, every sentence, every word must advance it.

A successful research project usually will give off many ideas. A new technique in teaching math may have implications for using statistics in social study and language acquisition. The way the math approach was successfully introduced to a resisting math department may have a lesson for school administrators. This may also produce a design for the retraining of teachers in a union-dominated school system. The method itself may have some implications for teachers of advanced students and quite different ones for brain-damaged students. It may incorporate a team-teaching technique and a new variation on evaluation. Most of all, it may clarify how we think through certain problems. The tendency is to jam everything into one article. The editor experienced with reaching a large audience would advise the educational researcher to publish a series of short articles, each one developing and documenting a research finding for a specific audience.

5. Emphasize the Positive

Inexperienced writers usually assume that the reader does not know the problem—classes are too large, teachers need retraining, there are students with learning disabilities in the classroom—and preach, telling the reader there is a problem. In fact, most of the time the reader knows the problem—Johnny can't spell "smel"—but doesn't know what to do about it.

The writer will reach a large audience if solutions are presented as well as problems. Spelling may not be learned in 284 schools, but it may be in Bear Paw School. The professional writer will concentrate on Bear Paw School. Writing which attracts readers shows a problem and its solutions. It tells the reader what can be done. It leaves the reader with something to do—try the techniques which work in Bear Paw School.

6. Short Is Harder - and Better

Many writers apologize for writing a long letter by saying they didn't have time to write a short one. It takes time—and courage—to produce a short piece of writing, because brevity is achieved by selection. Meaning is not jammed into a bouillon cube to produce brevity; the writer selects what is most important and develops each of those points efficiently but fully.

This requires an executive turn of mind. The writer must decide what is important and what can be left out. Brevity, of course, exposes the writer. It allows the reader to see just what the writer means, and academics, too often, are trained to play it safe. This results in communication—and exposure.

The influential readers that educational researchers must reach are busy. They simply will not read long, involved pieces of writing. Perhaps they should. The most responsible—and most guilty—will purchase, clip, copy, and put aside long, profound pieces to be read during Christmas break, or next summer, or on a sabbatical some time in the future. While those pieces grow into Alps of good intention, short, disciplined pieces of writing which get to the point in a hurry are read and have an impact.

7. Answer Your Readers' Questions—Especially If You Don't Want Them Asked

The writer must assume an intelligent ignorance on the part of the general public. The writer believes the reader does not know the subject but is capable of knowing it.

Probably the best way of anticipating what the audience needs to know is to write down the questions—the toughest questions—an uninformed but intelligent reader might ask.

The kinds of questions which the writer must ask of his own piece of writing might include:

- What are the results of this experiment with using computers to teach languages?
- Who chose the sample? Did that load the dice?
- Is the school typical?
- What does it mean for high school students?
- What needs to be done now?
- What are the problems teachers will have using the system?
- What will it cost?

These may not be the questions the writer wants asked, but they may be the questions an intelligent and skeptical audience will ask.

The writer often finds it helpful to ask these questions during the prewriting process before the first draft. These questions can become an outline or an organizational plan for the article or book, since the effective writer anticipates the reader's questions and answers them at the point they will most certainly arrive in the reader's mind.

8. Edit for Simplicity

The goal of writing should be simple clarity. The writer should not be visible. As George Orwell said, "Good prose is like a window pane." The reader's attention should be focused on the subject, not on the person presenting the subject. Not all ideas, of course, can be expressed with elementary simplicity. But each idea should be presented as simply as possible if the writer wants to achieve a general audience. Some of the tricks of the editor's trade include:

Write titles, not labels

A label simply says what it is: "A Test to Evaluate Mathematical Skills of Creative Writing Students." A title focuses, clarifies, and draws the reader in, "Killing a Myth: Poets Can't Calculate."

Obviously the title, far more than the label, helps the reader, but it also is of great importance to the writer, for each title is, in a sense, a draft. Often I will write a hundred titles during the prewriting process.

Each one limits the subject, helps me focus on it, and may even establish the voice with which the piece will be written.

Of course the title must be honest; it should not promise what the writer can not deliver.

Write leads, not introductions

The introduction tells the reader what you intend to say. The lead draws the reader right into the subject. The introduction gets between the reader and the subject; the lead is the subject evolving.

If you do not see the importance of writing effective leads, then have a friend go through a newspaper, magazine or journal and tell you when the decision is made to read on or turn to another article. In my experience that decision will be made in less than five seconds, in most cases less than three. Clearly the writer must realize that he or she has ten lines or less in which to capture and hold the reader.

The discipline of the lead, however, is not only a service to the reader, it is an opportunity for the writer. As the title helps the writer focus on the subject, so does the lead. The lead eliminates much of what might intrude upon the subject. It focuses, it establishes the dimensions of the piece. It often identifies the audience, and it sets the voice.

Skillful lead-writing is what makes it possible for the journalist to write clean copy in a brief period of time under pressure. The experienced journalist usually writes the lead on the way back to the office, and once the lead is set, the piece of writing flows. The hard news journalist lead is built on who, what, when, where, and why (or how). As the journalist becomes the magazine writer, or the book writer, the lead becomes even more important. I often write fifty leads, fifty first paragraphs, before starting the first draft. Sometimes the lead will come quickly, other times it will emerge only after a great deal of struggle. But most non-fiction writers find they must establish the lead before they go on. The lead gives them the approach to the piece of writing.

Let's see how a lead might evolve:

"It was established that the parameters of the writing program were less withdrawn than might have been predicted at the beginning of the testing program. One saw written communication in contextual situations in which it had not been hypothesized."

• • •

"The experiment was designed to show when students wrote within the Language Arts curriculum. Data revealed that students write as much or more during other elements of the learning experience."

• • •

"Writing isn't owned by Language Arts teachers. Writing is taught, learned, and practiced in all parts of the curriculum and outside of school as well. That was the result of a test program..."

• • •

"Muriel wrote a book report on Monday for her Language Arts teacher, a science report on Tuesday, and an imaginary explorer's account in Social Studies on Wednesday. After school on Wednesday, Muriel helped write a new class constitution. On Thurday she described a turtle trying to escape a tank. That night she wrote a thank-you note to her grandmother and then worked on a skit with four children from church. On Friday Muriel wrote a description for her Language Arts teacher. She said that was Muriel's second writing assignment for the week.

The Language Arts teacher thought she was the only writing teacher in the school. Research shows that writing is taught more by Social Studies and Science teachers than Langugae Arts teachers, perhaps even more in the home and the community than in the Language Arts classroom."

That last lead doesn't tell you what is going to be said, it draws you right into what is being said. It informs and attracts. And note how much it helps the writer. The subject of the article and, therefore its dimensions, its order, its development, its audience, its tone, pace, and voice are all made clearer by the lead.

Build with paragraphs

The paragraph is the basic unit of non-fiction. Each paragraph should be short, and it should move the piece of writing forward by developing a piece of information which the reader needs when the reader needs it. It is helpful to remember that the point of greatest emphasis is at the end of a paragraph, and the next most important point at the beginning. Information in the middle of the paragraph is not emphasized.

The greatest enemy to vigorous and effective paragraphs is the topic sentence (even though this is one). English teachers teach that a flat statement topic sentence must always be used. But this statement of what is to be said tends to get between the reader and the subject. Each paragraph should have a topic, but in most cases that topic should be implied, not stated.

Writers who are having difficulty organizing a piece of writing often find it helpful to draft a single paragraph to the page. This helps the writer develop each paragraph fully. Then, when all the paragraphs are drafted, the writer can spread them out on a desk, table, bed, or floor, and move them around until the writer discovers the simplest, most effective organization, the one which answers the reader's questions at the time that the reader asks them.

Respect the subject-verb-object sentence

The simple sentence seems too simple for many academics, but good writing for a general audience is constructed of sentences which are direct and vigorous. Of course, the effective writer varies the length and design of the sentence so that the sentences march before the reader in a pleasing and clarifying order. But the key points should be made in short, declarative sentences, and not hidden behind a hedgerow of clauses.

Avoid jargon

Jargon is the private language spoken between specialists. Specialists may argue that they use jargon because it is precise. But such precision—if it exists—is lost unless it is spoken between specialists in the same narrow area of knowledge. And, more and more, we can not stay within our narrow specialties. One group of computer programmers may speak the same jargon, but they deal with statisticians from psychology, sociology, political science, education, forest resources, and their jargon is blurred until it becomes meaningless. And when these people attempt to speak to the public the jargon becomes incomprehensible.

Most jargon is used to impress, not to communicate; to establish a professional club and exclude everyone else; to complicate, not to clarify.

We all have our special pet hates—parameters instead of limits, school practitioners instead of teachers, interface, finalize, interpersonal relationships, software, viability—each day seems to bring a new horror.

Language should be a precision instrument, and it can be if the writer looks at the subject and seeks the simplest, most direct word which communicates information. The important thing for the writer to remember is that he or she is writing with information, and that each word must carry information to the reader as efficiently as possible.

Write with verbs and nouns

Verbs are the machines that make writing move. The effective writer for the general public will write principally with active verbs and specific nouns. The writer feels that adverbs and adjectives imply failure, failure to find the right verb or the right noun.

Writers also seek the active voice rather than the passive. "John was hit by Jim" uses two more words but says no more than, "Jim hit John."

Cut everything that can be cut

A paragraph E. B. White quoted from William Strunk, Jr. in *Elements of Style* was framed over my desk for many years:

> "Vigorous writing is concise. A sentence should contain no unnecessary words, a paragraph no unnecessary sentences, for the same reason that a drawing should have no unnecessary lines and a machine no unnecessary parts. This requires not that the writer make all his sentences short, or

that he avoid all detail and treat his subjects only in outline, but that every word tell.''

The writer should have no greater joy, perhaps, than pruning a piece of writing, cutting out every word that can be cut out, changing constructions so that they are clearer, simpler, shorter, making the abstract concrete, the general specific, the complex clear.

Each writer will develop his own list of editorial enemies. Mine include quite, that, ings, would, the verb ''to be,'' transitional phrases. This list will change as the writer changes. Of course, these are stylistic choices (and, of course, of course should be on my list) and, of course, there will be times when they are appropriate, but they tend to clutter my page. You will have to identify your own clutter and then eliminate it.

9. Listen for Your Own Voice

Writing for a mass audience is still an individual act—one person speaking to another. Write as much as possible as you would speak. At least give the illusion of speech. And when you have a question about how to write something, read it aloud. Even the most prolific writer speaks far more than he or she writes. The ear is an effective editor.

A piece of writing which appeals to a general audience usually has a human, consistent voice. Effective, memorable writing is usually not impersonal and general, but specific and personal.

10. Break Any Rule

George Orwell's final rule in ''Politics and the English Language'' was ''Break any of these rules sooner than say anything outright barbarous.'' The purpose of clear writing is clarity and communication, not etiquette. Any rule can and should be broken if it helps to clarify and communicate the meaning. And no rule should be followed if it impedes the clarification of meaning.

One of the greatest impediments to effective writing is the way writing has been taught by English teachers. Language is alive. It changes with the seasons. Grammarians try to contain it, but they can not. Language can't be imprisoned in any rule book. There is, in fact, little agreement between some of the principal rulebooks and between the teachers who use them. The writer should not follow rules, but follow language towards meaning, always seeking to understand what is appearing on the page, to see it clearly, to evaluate it clearly, for clear thinking will produce clear writing.

As in ice skating, it's easier to say how to write than to write. Educational researchers can, however, learn to write clear prose which will be read by classroom teachers, principals, superintendents, taxpayers, parents, and schoolboard members. Writing for the general public is not an art, but a craft; not a mystery, but a discipline which can be understood and learned if it is practiced. Then the results of educational research may reach the classroom and improve the education of our children.

III

The Process of Teaching

I look back on this article as a fine example of chutzpah. Five years a teacher, and this my first article on teaching. But then I realize that this is the same year in which *A Writer Teaches Writing* was published—a textbook on teaching yet.

In my defense I can only say that in my first semester of teaching I was assigned teachers to teach. We learned together as I taught what I was learning. But I expected that process to end. It hasn't.

16
Give Your Students the Writer's Five Experiences

The other day a young high school teacher asked me, "I've been assigned to a writing course this fall, what should I teach?"

"You don't teach anything," I answered. "You let the students write, you read what they've written with the class, and then you each try to help each of them say what he has to say."

It was good advice, the distillate of what is practiced in university writing workshops across the country. But it was unfair to give the young lady such a quick answer. The beginning English teacher—or the experienced English teacher who is inexperienced in teaching writing—needs more than such glib counsel, for we are all taught the virtues of lesson plans, syllabi and course outlines. We gripe about them, but still depend on them. I know that I certainly lean on a lesson plan, and the more inexperienced I am in teaching a course, the more heavily I lean.

As teachers we are taught to prepare lessons to bring to our students. We see ourselves as beasts of intellectual burden who haul fact, interpretation, commentary, analysis, and information into the classroom to dump it on the student.

This does not work in the writing course, because there is no great body of knowledge to lug into the class. There are only a relatively few simple principles, constantly reborn out of the writer's experience—recurrent problems and recurrent solutions. And these principles of writing not only seem irrelevant to the student, they are indeed irrelevant until he discovers them for himself in solving his own writing problems.

Published in *The Leaflet,* November, 1968.

Teaching writing has its peculiar difficulties. For example, you can rarely prepare a class and therefore you feel as if you come to the class naked. This, of course, is not the case. You bring all that you know to class so that it can be brought to bear, spontaneously, on the problems faced by individual writers on the page. The writing teacher must be prepared to diagnose the student writer's problems and to respond to them. The students must be forced to take the initiative in the writing course. The course is most successful when students discover their own problems, and when they discover their own solutions. You, the teacher, create a climate in which this process can take place and you succeed the most when you interfere—or teach—the least.

Writing is a skill, or an art, and, therefore, the composition course is a laboratory or workshop course. You can't learn to write by reading before the fact, by discussion before the fact, by critical analysis after the fact, or by lecture before or after the fact of writing. These are all valid teaching techniques, part of the writing teacher's arsenal. But the emphasis in the course must be on what the student is doing, for writing simply can not be taught theoretically, in the abstract. Writing must be experienced to be learned.

This teaching role in which the teacher responds instead of initiating does not threaten the status of the shop teacher, the art teacher, the music teacher, the science lab teacher or the football coach. But it does seem to frighten and threaten the English teacher who too often envisions himself as a modern Moses who brings the tablets, possibly Xeroxed for class distribution, down from the mountain each day. The English teacher's model is usually, unfortunately, his college English professor, and therefore he feels guilty if he, the teacher, is not continually talking. I am an English professor, and I certainly do love to talk, but I am convinced that listening is an inefficient educational procedure most of the time, at least in the writing course.

We also have an understandable tendency to over-organize our courses. Perhaps we want to impress our superiors, our colleagues, our students, or just to give ourselves a sense of security. We plan to teach diction in the third week in September, iambic pentameter in October, parallel construction in November, the essay in December, description in January, footnotes in February—everything neatly organized into some pattern which seems rational to the teacher in advance of the beginning of school. I am a great organizer, and my course outlines are a matter of enormous pride and satisfaction to me. I scatter them about me as if they were rose petals of purple ditto. When I began to teach, after years of being a full time writer, I didn't know what to teach or how to teach it, but I did know how to make outlines. Each year, however, my outlines have become less formal because I have traveled from school to school during the past few years and seen hundreds of lesson plans which are often impressive, usually contradictory, and almost always irrelevant to what the successful teacher is doing in class. In the writing course the course outline is a crutch which should be discarded as soon as the students begin to write. As they write and reveal their composition problems the students design their own course. That is the way it should be, and the professional teacher should be flexible enough to teach the course his particular students need this term, not the course he planned or hoped to teach.

But what is the teacher to do at the beginning of the term if the writing course starts not when the teacher talks but when the students write? The teacher spends his time creating an environment in which a student can work, and discipline under which he must work, and then the teacher enters into the course with his students by writing himself.

It is terrifying to reveal yourself to your pupils by trying to practice what you've been preaching, but once a teacher engages in the writing process with his students he will never be the same again. Writing teachers are fortunate to be able to share the excitement of learning with our students. We too can pass through the five experiences of the writer. We don't hide behind our desks but sit down with our students and write. Afterwards we sit beside them and accept their criticism while they accept ours. And then we all go back to rewrite.

In this process each writing course recreates itself. Each year is new, each class is new, for the process of writing can never be perfected. There is always a new challenge, a new discovery, and there is no satisfaction in teaching to be compared to the excitement of entering into the educational experience of your students, forever young, forever learning. You can share your students' intellectual explorations of the five basic experiences of the writer.

The Experience of Seeing

The first experience of the writer which the student writer should share is the experience of seeing. The writer has to see to have something to say. Before anything else, the writing course is the practice of perception. The teacher may demonstrate what it means to see, using photographs, a tour of the school, and his own observations for demonstration. He may expand the perception to other senses, using records, odors, textures, to make the student aware of his own world. He may also read, or have the students read, excerpts from literature which show the writer's awareness of his world, as long as the teacher realizes that literature is only one way of viewing the world. It may be the best way for the teacher, but it may not be the most effective way for the average student.

At first the experience of seeing may only be expressed through lists of specifics—describe a person or a place, with 25, 100, or 250 specifics. Such exercises help the student feel the writer's awareness which produces the raw materials for his writing.

Eventually the student may move from description to analysis and to theoretical writing using the same technique of listing specifics, for the scholar or the scientist first collects his evidence or his data, and then, as it accumulates and begins to assume a pattern of its own, he begins to discover evolving meaning. This process is similar to a photograph slowly appearing developer. The writer begins to see the meaning through the specifics which he has collected. First, however, the student writer has to see, and the teacher's task is to create an atomosphere and an attitude which will encourage the student to see.

The Experience of Form

The second experience is the artist's fundamental experience of form. The writer experiences form as he feels the irrelevant becoming relevant, the random assuming pattern, the apparently pointless unrelated fact pointing toward meaning. The writer—the artist—brings order to disorder. Form may be a story, a letter,a scientific report, a paragraph, a novel, a scene, a list—anything which makes sense of the multiple impressions which our brain collects from both the library book and the conversation on the street corner.

The artist doesn't so much admire form as he hungers for it. He needs form to give him meaning. His business is to design ideas into thoughts, and the student writer must learn to organize his perceptions. He should be free to toy with his facts, since the writer may be most disciplined when he is most playful, teasing a meaning out of evidence which once seemed irrelevant or contradictory.

Once the student has built a form for himself which stands up to a critical reader he will never be quite the same again. Form is something you—and the reader—can hold on to, something that makes it possible for a reader to recognize your meaning. The student writer must make his own paragraph, poem, report, or story which has successful form. He must know the sense of completeness the writer feels when he has made something which was not there before, when he has experienced form.

The Experience of Publication

Next, the student writer must suffer the exciting, terrifying experience of publication. The writer is the man revealed by the printing press. All others escape but the writer's words are examined coldly by an objective audience. We see how well he writes, and by seeing how he writes we see how he thinks. Indeed, we see what he is.

The printing press waits, and in the writing course its deadline should be irrevocable. Everything may be avoided except the moment of publication. The printing press may, of course, be a ditto machine, a real printing press, carbon paper, a bulletin board, a mimeograph, a xerox, an overhead projector, but there must come a time when the student writer has his own words wrenched from him so they appear naked before his own eye, apart from apologies and explanations, good intentions and sincere promises.

The writing course moves forward because the student faces the same discipline as the writer: the arbitrary deadline. It may be the end of the hour, the end of the day, the end of the week, but the student must face a frequent, inflexible deadline. Score is kept, and the student must deliver a draft or a revision. The subject, the form, the length may and should be his, but the deadline is the publisher's. There is an hour when the work, at last, must be passed in and the writer revealed. The teacher may vary the deadline or even change it in special cases, but the editor knows the professional will not deliver unless he faces a deadline and the copy is taken from him. Writing is never completed; the process of revision, reconsideration and editing goes on until the final deadline is met.

Then, when the deadline has passed and the writer is published, he is tested. Publication is the writer's big game, the concert hall recital, the opening night, the combat fire fight, and the writing student has to be bloodied if he is to learn. He has to suffer the awful revelation of what he has said compared to what he meant to say.

The Experience of Communication

The student should also, before the composition course is over, have the experience of communication. Few students have enjoyed good listeners at home or at school, and yet we all have the basic need for communication and understanding. We laugh at the trite complaint "My wife doesn't understand me." But often in cliches lie truth. We all want to be understood, to communicate our dreams and our fears, our hopes and our apprehensions, our experiences and the implications we see in them.

Once the student has found an audience he will catch fire. He will be motivated to write once the basic satisfaction of communication has been given to him, and this is where the teacher plays his most important role. The teacher creates an environment in which the student finds an audience of his peers and in which the audience of his peers has been trained to respond constructively to a piece of writing in process.

The teacher, however, should be the class's most expert reader. He should perceive, through the confusion of the student's writing, the potential meaning. He is able to diagnose the student's fundamental problem and to prescribe possible solutions which the student may try. He is never, however, the final reader. He should always think of himself as a coach or a tutor or an adviser who is helping the student to speak to his own audience. The student writer will, and should, suspect the teacher's reaction. The student must discover he can communicate to his own audience.

The Experience of Failure

Finally, the student must learn to live with the most important writer's experience of all: the experience of failure. We live in a success-oriented society, and it is hard for the student and the student's parents to understand that the writer always fails, but he uses failure in the process of writing. Failure is never pleasant, but too often it is essential. Sometimes the first draft may be the final draft, but usually the writer tries to say something, and fails, and through failure tries to say it better, and fails, but perhaps, eventually, he says it well enough. The writing course is an experimental course. It is a course in process, a course in practicing, a course in trying, a course in choice, a course in craft. Failure should not be accepted passively, but failure should never be defeat. The student should learn to exploit his failures as he rediscovers his subject, re-researches his information, redesigns his form, rewrites and edits every sentence.

What shall I teach this fall in my writing courses? As always, I approach the first day with a sense of inadequacy, a sense of apprehension, and a most exciting sense of anticipation. I do not know what I will teach, but I do know what my students will learn. Slowly, at first, the class will begin to hear some individual voices speak. And we will listen to these voices and try to help them become more effective, more confident.

My students will begin to learn how to write, not because of what I will tell them, but because of what they will experience. They will experience sight, they have something to say; they will experience form, and discover how to say it; they will experience publication, and become writers; they will experience communication and know they can reach at least one other human being; they will experience failure and begin to discover the craft of writing. They will, in just a few weeks, pass through the five experiences of the writer and begin to teach themselves to write.

As I worked with teachers I kept hearing the refrain, "My students won't revise." But when I went into classrooms where revision was not seen as a punishment, but an opportunity, I saw students eager to revise. In this article I tried to show why students like to revise, and how they can be encouraged to revise.

17
Teach the Motivating Force of Revision

Revision—the process of seeing what you've said to discover what you have to say—is the motivating force within most writers. They are compelled to write to see what their words tell them.

Revision can also be the motivating force within students—if they are given the opportunity to experience the adventure of rewriting. Unfortunately most language arts and English teachers do not appreciate the importance or the excitement of revision. They teach rewriting—if they teach it at all—as punishment, the price you have to pay if you don't get it right the first time.

But few, if any writers ever get it right the first time. They write to catch a glimpse of what they may see and then revise—and revise and revise and revise—to make it come clear. Jules Feiffer talks of writing *Knock, Knock:* "I had nothing particular in mind, so I did what actors do when they improvise, I put two people in a room and had them start talking."[1]

It is the mystery, the suspense and the surprise that pulls the writer forward. "I feel the same excitement a reader feels," Jessamyn West explains, "because my characters say and do things I don't know they are going to say and do."[2] Larry McMurty adds, ". . . the writing of a book is the process of finding out how it turned out that way."[3]

Since the writer doesn't know what the pen is going to put on the page, the first task of revision is vision. The writer must stand back from the work the way any craftsman does to see what has been done. The writer reads with wonder and with care to find out what the page may be saying. Writers often know more clearly what they don't want to say than what they do. "Artists don't always know what they are doing, but they are usually aware of what they are not doing." Robert Motherwell continues, "What I reject, I'm conscious of. What I'm striving for is only dimly perceived."[4]

Published in *English Journal,* October, 1978.

This process of moving towards meaning implies a continual process of revision. Writers have to see what is on the page and then decide to cut, change, or keep it. Economist John Kenneth Galbraith states, "...there are days when the result is so bad that no fewer than five revisions are required. In contrast, when I'm greatly inspired, only four revisions are needed."[5]

We are beginning to understand that the role of discovery is crucial to effective writing—in technical reports as well as poems, political essays as well as short stories, research papers as well as movie scripts. Sheridan Baker points out, "...the process of writing is a process of discovery. Everyone who writes has experienced this process, has discovered through writing it out, what he has in mind. Yet this simple fact is one not frequently propounded in our textbooks."[6]

Richard L. Larson emphasizes the importance of this process, "The power of making discoveries—of drawing connections between bits of experience so that they reveal or point to new ideas and problems, of asking questions in such a way that they can be answered with fresh insights into a subject—is, I suggest, one of the powers that makes education possible. Without it, the student is an assimilator of knowledge, a sponge soaking up and occasionally releasing information supplied by others. With it, the student can make independent sense of the diverse experiences that he or she encounters in college and outside, and can even operate on what we sometimes call the frontiers of knowledge. I suggest that English, particularly the teaching of composing, look toward giving the students the ability to make discovery."[7]

Larson goes on, quite properly, to praise the important work which has been done on invention and prewriting. He does not mention the work being done connecting the process of discovery with the processes of revision, rewriting and editing probably because very little work is being done in this area. Yet it often seems to the writer that the most important discoveries are made during the process of revision.

There are two forms of revision—one internal and one external. Internal revision occurs when writers are trying to find out what they have to say; external revision when they know what they have to say and are revising or editing their work so it can be understood by another audience. These two forms of revision, of course, overlap, but I believe they are distinct and significant. Writers must first understand what they are saying if others are to understand what was said.

Revision can be dull work indeed if the writer is only trying to conform to a particular set of editorial conventions, if the process of discovery is concluded and there are no surprises lurking on the page. But that is not revision. Writers find their writing alive under their pens. What they have to say is continually evolving beneath the hand.

What a motivating force this is. As writers, we are drawn forward to see what argument comes forth in our essays, to find out if hero becomes victim in our novels, to discover the reasons for an historic event in our biographies, to experience the image which makes a blurred snapshot in our memory come clear in our poems. I once received a magazine assignment to write a report on the elderly imprisoned in county homes. It was never written, but I have published a novel which has taken me inside the body of a young man who is a quadraplegic, who cannot move his arms or his legs. I set out to write a piece of journalism and found a novel. It could as easily have gone the other way. The writer is continually surprised by where language leads.

I face a pad of paper and find myself writing of a black bird which seems to fly through a tree outside my study window and find myself more than two years later, having taken a trip into my past where I meet my parents in a series of poems, understanding them a bit better than I ever did while they were alive.

Will the reader share my understanding? I hope so, but that is a small matter. No reader's response, no publication or award will come close to the explorations and discoveries I have made, all unexpected and unpremeditated, within the writing process while I am alone at my desk in the early morning. In rewriting and rewriting this article I have not reported what I knew about the teaching of rewriting as much as I have thought through an important irony: Most teachers are convinced, in advance, that their poorest students will refuse to rewrite while actually the strongest force to motivate those reluctant writers may be the act of revision. Of course I want to communicate this opinion in this article, but I must admit the greatest satisfaction is in making these small, personal statements to myself, not in publishing them. The older I get the longer completed manuscripts rest on my desk, not because I am shy but because once the discovery has been made by me to me, I am on to new territory in other pieces of writing.

Teachers who have not experienced this process of discovery through language we call writing are convinced their students will not want to rewrite. And they will not, if those teachers communicate rewriting as punishment. And yet these same teachers, when they do a paper in a course, feel they could do better if only they had another chance. The process-centered writing curriculum gives students that other chance.

Most students, in fact, find this other chance—this opportunity to rewrite—as exciting to them, even as necessary to them, as it is to writers. Writing is no longer a matter of rules or exercises. It is what they do to find out something about themselves or something about a subject in which they are interested. Students, like writers, will be driven to revise—to read and rewrite—in order to find out what they have to say.

And the force which motivates the student to write may motivate the teacher who has previously dreaded the pile of completed writing assignments. As the student begins to make discoveries on the page, the writing teacher has the privilege of sharing those discoveries. The teacher is not reading assignments which are, at best, predictable and fulfilled; the writing teacher shares the excitement of the unexpected subject, the evolving form, the astonishment of the word that is almost wrong and exactly right.

Yesterday a student asked me in conference, "What are you doing?" It was a fair question, I was dressed in what passes for University of New Hampshire faculty style—L. L. Bean shirt and Dunham boots—leaning back in my chair, feet on my desk, chatting about old cars and how he felt about them. It might not seem that I was doing anything, and he was paying for the course out of his own pocket.

"I'm following your piece of writing."

He looked puzzled.

"To see where it may take you."

"But I'm kind of tired of it. I don't know if I want to write about that old Volvo any more."

"Fine. No need to. I'm just kind of interested in that guy who is so involved in that car he can describe it in hundreds of details. I can see the car now, in this draft, but I'm getting more interested in the guy who saw a vision of a fine car in that rusty hunk of junk. It might be a story."

We sit quietly for a couple of minutes.

"But I can't write a story."

"What do you mean?"

"Well I don't know exactly what I want to say. I haven't got any themes. I mean writing fiction, you have to know so much." He draws a huge map in the air, "Like Tolstoy. A whole world. How everything fits in."

We chat about how writers discover what they have to say, how little they know, how essential is my ignorance of what happens in the next chapter of the novel I am drafting. I point out that he may discover an article on rebuilding junk cars, on mechanics who gouge the unsuspecting, on how to save money repairing a car. We even discuss the possibility of a girl who waves to the fellow working on the car which makes him write a story in which there is no Volvo at all. Our fifteen minutes is up. He turns at the door, "What do you want me to do?"

"Write."

"Well, what? What do you expect me to do?"

"Whatever you want. I want to be surprised. You don't know what you're going to write, how can I know? It wouldn't be any fun if I did."

Well, what will he do? I really do not know. I can make no prediction and would not if I could. That is the fun in teaching writing. He will write something; that is required. More than likely, he will write what he does not expect to write. The subject or the form or the language will change under his hand. It will surprise him and it will surprise me. That is why I turn eagerly to my students' papers. Not to correct them, never to correct them—that is their job—but to find out what they have to say, to see their worlds through their eyes.

In one day I read the papers of dozens of students and in conference share with them the experience of finding subjects which are new to them, of recreating the old forms of literature in a way that serves their needs in making our language their language.

That is also the reason I prefer to teach beginning students, especially remedial students. The reluctant writers have no idea of the importance and excitement of writing, no suspicion that rewriting will let them see their worlds more clearly than they ever have before by using the lens of language.

In teaching beginning students there is no content in the writing course until they put it in. All the teaching is responsive. Perhaps they only list specifics at first, but they write. And as they put down the concrete details about their world, usually starting with description, they begin to see the world in a way they have never seen it before.

This becomes apparent to them and to their teacher, because the teacher first asks each student what the student thinks of the paper. There are generally two responses.

The student may be surprised at finding out what appeared during the process of rewriting. The student may never have heard of Robert Frost who said, "For me the initial delight is the surprise of remembering something I didn't know I knew." With the student, it may come out, "Well, gee, I mean, it was kinda like, I mean, well, you know, I never thought of it that way, it was different sort of not what I expected." Don't worry about the syntax. That student is hooked on writing.

The beginning student is more likely not to be aware of any discovery on the page. Most students do not think they have anything to say and the tragedy is that their teachers agree with them. It is the job of the writing teacher to find what is on the page which may be hidden from the student. It may be a word that has potential ("I was enlarged when the bully came after my sister."), an interesting and potentially significant fact ("Bird watchers like pollution. They know some pollution is good for birds."), a phrase that rubs two unexpected words together and gives off a meaning ("My mother was taught to be a lady. She can softly slam a door."), a point of view ("Sometimes it seems like the smaller and poorer the houses, the bigger the churches.").

The writing teacher may not be able to locate the potential in the language on the page but may just hear a tone of voice, feel a sense of humor or a sense of rage, recognize a potential area of authority. It is good enough, in the beginning to respond to that.

"Sounds to me like you've got a real gripe with motorcycle manufacturers."

"You know it."

"Well, tell me about it. It sounds interesting. Something people ought to know."

"O.K."

The potential may not even be on the page or anywhere near it. Then it is the job of the writing teacher to draw out of the student an area in which the student is an authority or could become an authority.

"What do you think of your paper?"

"I dunno."

"Did you find anything out in writing it?"

"Nope."

"What do you do outside of school?"

"Hang around."

"Where?"

"At a fillin' station. The Amoco on Hancock Street."

"Interested in cars?"

"Nope."

"Well, what happens at the station?"

"Not much."

"Nothing interesting?"

"Well, these guys came in the other night, asked me to go for a ride with 'em."

"Well?"

"You read about it in the papers. They killed a guy. I didn't know they had a gun."

"Why didn't you go with them?"

"I don't know. Too lazy I guess. I've wondered about it."

"Could you wonder on paper?"

"I guess."

That happened to me. Not as a teacher. As a student. But no teacher ever drew it out of me—but they could have. And if they had, I might have graduated from high school. There is potential even in the most unlikely student, and it may take a teacher all of ten minutes to tap it. The potential might have been realized in a series of drafts exploring a casual decision made during a boring teenage evening.

It is worth noting that the teacher should *not* command rewriting. In fact, the teacher may rarely use such words as revision or rewriting. The teacher expresses interest in the subject the student is writing and the student discovers, without realizing it, what Gore Vidal describes, "I am an obsessive rewriter, doing one draft then another and another, usually five. In a way, I have nothing to say, but a great deal to add."

Lack of development—an unsufficient amount of information—is the writer's primary problem. The professional writer learns this from editors and readers (usually with great resistance and complaint—writers know what they have said, why don't readers know it?) but a sufficient amount of information can be drawn out of the student writer by a patient and skillful writing teacher. The students, at first, become unconscious rewriters and later put a name to what has become an essential and rewarding part of the writing process. First the student must experience the excitement of discovery, later understand the process which produced the discovery. The student writes drafts before calling them drafts.

How does the teacher learn to spot the potential which lies within a student's writing or a student's experience so the teacher can encourage discovery? By being a writer. This does not mean that writing teachers should be Writers, with a capital W. It does mean they should frequently use language in a search for meaning; have recently experienced firsthand the terrror and joy of putting words on paper. The single most dramatic change that can be made in a language arts or English teacher who wants to teach writing is for the teacher to write with the students.

It is hard to imagine a music teacher who has never made music, or an art teacher who has never drawn a picture but, unfortunately, it is normal to have writing teachers who have written only academic papers—and shockingly few of those. The great majority of "writing" teachers have never written a story or a poem, never felt language leading them across the page.

The teacher should write with the student, showing the student how badly the writer writes, revealing the failures and mistakes and stupidities and awkwardness that clumsily lead the writer toward meaning, a meaning the writer did not expect, perhaps did not even want to accept. The teacher writes beside the student, the way the oboe teacher plays along with the student oboist, sharing the challenge of their art.

The big problem in the development of effective writing teachers is that most language arts and English teachers have been trained as reading teachers, literary critics, or, occasionally, students of the science of language. Most have been excused from freshman English, which is not usually a writing course; few have ever taken a course in writing or the teaching of writing. They are fans, not players; critics, not participants.

If students are to learn to write, then the writing teachers must cross over from the role of critic to player. The worst model for the writing class is for the teacher to be standing at the front of the room talking; the best model is for the teacher to be sitting at the rear of the room writing.

There are real hazards when teachers apply critical or scholarly tools to the product of writing in an effort to teach writing. They may, for example, tell the student, "You have to know what you want to say before you say it." We have all heard teachers say this. It seems logical if you have spent your time in examining the well-made products of literature. But it may be a misconception which makes it impossible for the students to write well. The fact is that most writers, most of the time, do not know what they want to say before they say it. Some may not even know what they have said after they have said it. Writing is not necessarily built by accretion, but scholarship. It may be the piling up of blocks, but it may also be the shooting of an arrow at a moving target only dimly perceived.

The untruths about the writing process, however, may be less important than the attitude the non-writing writing teacher brings to class. The teacher with sharp critical or scholarly tools may deal in absolutes, inhibiting or limiting the student writer. The writing teacher who writes, on the other hand, may be able to enter into the process of individual exploration with each student. The teacher who is experiencing important and surprising discoveries through language is likely to share and support each student's individual exploration of the world. The discoveries they make together are the energizing force which drives the writing course forward.

Because of this force, the teacher becomes less important towards the end of the writing course. The students have the scent of their own meanings. They are off and the teacher is not leading but hurrying after them, trying to keep up. The students are driven to write by the motivating force of revision, of reading what they have written to discover what they have to say.

References

[1]*New York Times,* February 10, 1976, p. 42.
[2]*Fiction! Interviews with Northern California Novelists,* ed. Dan Tooker and Roger Hofheins (New York: Harcourt Brace Jovanovich/William Kaufman, 1976), pp. 185-186.
[3]*Christian Science Monitor,* February 5, 1976.
[4]*New York Times,* February 3, 1976, p. 33.
[5]*Christian Science Monitor,* December 9, 1976.
[6]"Writing as Discovery," *ADE Bulletin,* November 1974, p. 34.
[7]"English: An Enabling Discipline," *ADE Bulletin,* September 1975, p. 5.

Most of the poor writing we see in schools is a direct result of the assignments given the students. Teachers, however, are dependent on assignment-giving, and they fear what will happen if they eliminate assignments. What happens, of course, is better writing.

18
What, No Assignments?

"But I don't have anything to say," is the most prevalent and most serious problem in the writing program. If the student has nothing to say, then there is no program. If the student isn't interested in Shakespeare there may still be a unit on Shakespeare, for the teacher can talk and talk and talk. But if there is no student writing there is no writing program, for student writing is the text of the writing program.

Since this problem is crucial, most English teachers who teach writing spend their lives in a search for good assignments, confident that somewhere there is a teacher with the magic, entire-class-stimulating assignment. But when they find a good assignment it doesn't quite work. There's good reason for this, for the assignment is not the solution to a lack of student writing, it is usually the cause.

Students will write well only when they speak in their own voice, and that voice can only be authoritative and honest when the student speaks of his own concerns in his own way.

The assignment means to help, but it hinders. We laugh at the mother who continues to dress her children long after they could do the job themselves, for we know she wants to keep her children babies. The assignment-giving teacher, who is also wrapped in virtue, does the same thing.

The good assignment and the poor assignment are often equally bad. They both inhibit the student from learning how to think and how to find his own subject. The assignment rewards the student without self-respect who is willing to con the teacher, because once he has the assignment he knows what the teacher wants; it also penalizes the student who has independence, his own mind and self-respect, for he is criticized when he doesn't deliver what the teacher expects from the assignment.

Published in *Alberta English,* Winter, 1973-74.

The teacher who doesn't want to teach writing but who wants his students to learn how to write has to understand what a good subject is, why his students have trouble finding subjects, and how they can find their own subjects.

Elements of a Good Subject

To the writer a good subject is what he has to write. "The urge to write poetry," says Robert Penn Warren, "is like having an itch. When the itch becomes annoying enough, you scratch it." You may discover you have writers in your class if your students see that writing is a response to their own concerns about their life. They may have an itch they'll have to scratch.

As they write, topics will evolve which have the three marks of a good subject: *content, form,* and *response.*

Content is composed of information and authority. The writer has something that he knows about. He has facts or feelings to communicate to the reader. Not words first, but something to say first, which can be symbolized by the words. First comes the experience, then comes the words.

The information leads to the vital sense of authority. Content is not just detached information, it is information which the author cares about, which he has a point of view towards, which he feels is important. The reader should recognize in the writer's content an author who knows what he is talking about and cares what he is talking about.

Form is the vehicle which communicates the writer's knowing and feeling. Form implies something more than content, that there isn't just the possibility of a subject but that there is a subject which can be limited by a form. It is a picture which has a frame, a game which has a ninth inning, a political campaign with an election.

An effective form—the lyric poem, the dramatic scene, the winning argument—does more than serve the content. It adds to the content, strengthening it and deepening it. Content is the raw material and form its realization. Remember, you can't assign form and then seek content; content predicts the form. What the writer has to say determines how he will say it.

Response means that the subject will do something for a reader or to a reader. Writing with content and form but no response may be good therapy for the writer, but the effective subject sparks a response in another human being.

The good subject breaks out of its isolation. The short story writer, for example, may be as Frank O'Connor has said, "A lonely voice." But once written and captured in a good subject, that voice isn't lonely any more. The good subject carries with it impact, "the shock of recognition."

Why Students Don't Find Subjects

There are eight principal reasons students don't find their own subjects, and they grow out of an academic atmosphere which does not allow the student to find his own subject. The writing teacher must create an academic climate which encourages, not discourages, each student's individual search for his own subjects.

The student writers are often *unaware,* but writing begins with perception, and the writing courses must allow time for the student to develop his senses and to realize the importance of his perceptive skills in writing. The girl who can see a dress in a store window and reproduce it at home, or the boy who can read a basketball defense while racing down the floor may not be dull in class if they are shown that their accomplished ability to see is the primary skill they use in the writing course. The rewards of the writing course should not be given to those who can use words so much as to those who can see things in the world which need words. As Joseph Conrad said, "My task. . . is, by the power of the written word, to make you hear, to make you feel—it is, before all, to make you see." The student writer must be open to his world, seeing it, feeling it, if he is to write about it.

Knowledge is essential for good writing, but most students don't know very much, at least about what they are forced to write in school. The writer—even the poet—writes with information. The student has to know something to say something, and you don't know very much after looking something up in the World Book at 10:30 the night before a paper is due. The student must grub around in his own experience and honestly explore his own world.

The student frequently lacks *self-respect,* and no one will write without some respect for his own voice. Too often in school we encourge the student's self-hate rather than his self-love. But no student will write well unless he believes he has something to say. This belief begins back before content. He must feel he has worth before he will say something of worth.

Honesty is essential to good writing, but honesty is not tolerated in the classroom—or too often at home or on the street corner. The student who writes to give the teacher what the teacher wants will write pap; whether it gets an "A" or a "D," it is still pap.

Writing is *thinking;* it is an intellectual act. Writing is not done with the emotions or with booze or grass, no matter what the romanticists think. Writing is done with the brain muscle; writing requires hard, skeptical, searching, self-critical thought that takes both time and effort.

The student's fear of *expsoure* is justified. The student doesn't want to put himself on the page because he will *BE* on the page, and he is right. Ignorance, arrogance, lack of charity, insensitivity—are all laid bare even on the page of the most objective prose. A person cannot be one kind of person and be another kind of writer. He is as good a writer as he is a person; when he writes he reveals himself. And the student writer must write in an environment which makes him willing to reveal himself, for there is no such thing as non-revealing writing.

A related impediment to good student writing is fear of *failure.* Our schools are success-oriented but you can only learn to write by committing yourself to what you may not be able to do. By not doing it you may see how you can do it the next time round. The writing curriculum must be failure-centered. The student must see the need for failure, and he must discover how to exploit it. The writer can never be the person who plays it safe, merely repeating last week's or last grade's success.

Finally, students don't find a subject because they don't *write*. You don't write down a subject you already know, you write to discover your subject. The girl who stays home every Saturday night is not likely to find a husband, and the writer who does not attempt a page will not find his subject. The writer writes to find out what he has to say, and if he writes he will discover not only how little he knows in some areas, but how much he knows in others. The writer explores his own mind by writing, and his fundamental excitement was best expressed by Robert Frost, who said, "For me the initial delight is in the surprise of remembering something I didn't know I knew."

How Students Can Find Subjects

The teacher, even in a self-contained classroom in a traditional school, can have students who will find their own subjects if that teacher emphasizes perception, allows time for free-writing, creates the possibility of publication, and puts the final responsibility of finding a subject right on the student.

In the beginning of the writing unit the teacher should emphasize *perception*. The writer's subjects come from his awareness of the world, and the potential writer needs time to exercise his senses. He has to discover how to record what he sees about him, perhaps at first with camera or tape-recorder, but soon with words, those symbols of language we use to stand for life.

The student should be encouraged to record long lists of specifics—precise, concrete observations. He can use these in a journal, on sheets of paper or file cards; the important thing is that he exercise each sense to record what he sees, feels, and thinks, and that he return later to these lists to find out how those specifics can spark memories he didn't know he had.

The teacher should involve himself in this game of exploration, sharing with the students his own discoveries and his own response to them. The student should learn not only to see, but to see honestly, and he should discover the excitement of hearing another person's honest voice.

Soon the student should be forced to perform *free writing*. Isn't that a contradiction in terms? Yes. And in my own class there is always an escape valve, but the more I teach the more I realize that I must make escape difficult. There is a deadline. There is an expectation of quantity, a demand for drafts. The student must be forced to face the blank page, for inspiration comes when you are writing, not thinking about writing.

Freedom, yes freedom of subject, freedom of opinion and conclusion, freedom of form and length, but not freedom from the deadline. The emphasis should be on writing. Quantity in the beginning, then perhaps quality will come. As Jules Renard said, "Talent is a question of quantity. Talent does not write one page: it writes 300."

The student must have time for day-dreaming, for dawdling, for writing drafts in his head. There must be allowances for individual differences, for one student thinks and then writes while another writes and then thinks. There must be a chance for those who write short and those who write long, for those who write many drafts and those who write few. But all students should share the pressure of production. You learn to write by writing: you find your own subject by seeing it appear under your own hand on your own page.

The student must experience *publication.* This means simply that he must be given the opportunity to find an audience among his peers. We all learn best by facing those we respect the most, those who share our problems—our peers. Students should write for themselves, but they should show what they have written when they want to, to each other. It's not so much that they will learn from their peers' criticisms as that they are sparked, sometimes even inspired, by seeing what other people in the class can do.

There is nothing quite so exciting as to see writing come to life in a classroom and a student turn into a writer during the course of a year. This can happen and this will happen if your students publish—by reading each other's folders, by writing out a few copies using carbon paper, by seeing class writing on the overhead projector, by having copies reproduced by machine or typed by the girls in the commercial class. The method is not important, except that it be as simple as possible. The important thing is that the focus not be on what some long dead author did on the page, but what can be produced on the blank page in this classroom.

And you can share in this too. You can be something close to a peer, not quite an equal but something far better than a teacher if you write too, and thereby earn your right to read as one of them. If you do not just ask your students to commit themselves, but if you lead the way by committing yourself to honesty, clarity, and discovery you will share your students' experience and earn their respect. In fact, writing with your students is such a powerful force that that one activity alone can change and revitalize a classroom. It can even change and revitalize a teacher.

Put the Student on the Spot

I have described a student-centered classroom in which the students, and hopefully the teacher, write each year's text for the course together, fresh each year in its failures and solutions, in its problems and discoveries. But student-centered does not mean permissive. It does mean stripping away every impediment to learning, no matter how reassuring those impediments are to the teacher. The student-centered classroom is one in which the student has no excuse for getting off the hook. He has the opportunity, the terrible freedom to learn.

In the writing course or unit the student should have no assignments. That's too easy. When you give a student an assignment you do most of the work for him. He must be driven back on himself to find something to say and a way of saying it which will earn the respect of his classmates and his teachers.

Where does he go to find the subject? James Michener has said, "The writer's job is to dig down where he is. He must write about the solid, simple things of his own land." James Baldwin has also said. "One writes out of one thing only—one's own experience. Everything depends on how relentlessly one forces from this experience, the last drop, sweet or bitter, it can possibly give. This is the only real concern of the artist, to recreate out of disorder of life that order which is art."

This has happened, in advantaged class and disadvantaged class, with slow learners and fast learners, through all the socio-economic gradations of our complex society when students are given freedom from assignments, when they are told: "Find your own subject."

Creative writing is one of those terms that makes every writer cringe. It seems to argue for the encouragement of everything, the lowering of standards, the rewarding of the superficial and the decorative. But the term stays with us, and I made an attempt to deal with it.

19
Why Creative Writing Isn't - or Is

The other day, I met one of our best teachers coming out of his classroom, and he said, "I don't know why everyone complains about these students. I think they're simply great."

They are—for him. And that's the truth most of us try to hide with the cynicism of the faculty lounge. Our student's potential is there, but most of us don't potentiate it.

The creative writing teacher is particularly on the spot, for more and more people are discovering what the writer knows, that talent is plentiful, that most of us have far more talent than we ever realize. Now our colleagues are seeing printed evidence of our students' capabilities. A number of teachers of writing in this country and in Great Britain have published books and articles which demonstrate how well even the most disadvantaged students can write. Such teacher-writers as Herbert Kohl, David Holbrook, J. H. Walsh, Dan Fader, Sybil Marshall, Frank Whitehead, Sylvia Ashton-Warner, Stephen Joseph, Margaret Langdon, Budd Schulberg, Marie Peel, A. B. Clegg, Kenneth Koch, and many others have documented the talent which can be demonstrated through the creative writing of average school children. These books and articles leave us with a tough question: Why is so much creative writing taught and so little creative writing produced?

Of course we have to define creative writing. Like most writers I detest the term. Its connotation seems to imply precious writing, useless writing, flowery writing, writing that is a luxury rather than a necessity, something that is produced under the influence of drugs or leisure, a hobby. School teachers encourage this distinction by the use of such terms as "functional writing" or "objective writing" or "practical writing" for writing they consider not "creative." In fact, creative writing functions, can be objective, and is extremely practical.

Published in *Elementary English,* April, 1973.

There is, however, one distinction between the two classifications of writing that may stand up. Most writing simply communicates information. It tells a reader merely what he needs to know. That is a respectable goal, but some writing rises above this level; it not only communicates information, it makes the reader care about that information, it makes him feel, it makes him experience, it gets under his skin. That is what we call creative writing.The writer simply calls it good writing, writing that works. And if it gets under enough people's skin, generation after generation, it is art.

There are seven elements, or experiences, the writer goes through most of the time when he produces something which gets under the reader's skin. The writer may be a student or an old pro, he may wear a beard or a business suit, be female or black, write poetry or journalism, biography or a novel, a play or an essay, but if he makes the reader care, then he is a creative writer.

Everyone who produces creative writing—words which make the reader itch and scratch—must pass through these seven experiences.

Creative writing *isn't* because it can't be taught. You can't pour creativity into children's heads through conventional teaching methods. It won't pour. But a teacher can open the door to creativity if he encourages his students to discover who he is and what he has to say.

The teacher whose students produce creative writing understands the creative process and in a way that is consistent (honest) with his own personality, training and subject matter, establishes a climate in which his students can find their own way through the seven stages of creativity at their individual pace.

I Awareness

The creative writer is more exposed to life than most people. He is open, sensitive, and curious. He asks tough questions and accepts honest answers. Above all, he sucks up more specific information than most people—sounds, facts, observations, smells, quotations, the incredibly rich raw material of life.

II Caring

The creative writer is involved with what he learns about life. He is concerned. Life makes him bitter, happy, cyncial, hopeful, believing, skeptical, amused, and angry. He has sympathy, and that special kind of sympathy we call empathy. He can imagine what it is like to inhabit someone else's skin, what are the implications of an event. He wonders what if. . .and he cares.

III Incubation

The creative writer has a working respect for his subconscious. He is not afraid to allow his unthinking mind to play with unconventional combinations of information. He dreams, as we all do, but he remembers more of his dreams than most of us, and lives with what he has dreamt. He learns to allow time for his subconscious mind to work with the primitive materials of life, for he knows that something productive is taking place in the unfelt turbulence of his secret mind while his consciousness walks or sleeps or visits or reads.

IV Discovery

The most important single element in the creative writing process is discovery. The creative writer is a person who has to find his own meanings in life. His individuality doesn't come from words, but from the order he constructs from our mutual chaos. No matter how many people have gone before him, the writer has an ego, a self-respect, or a self-centeredness which forces him to ask his own questions and find his own answers. He has to explore the reason which lies behind his own life, and he uses his craft to create that order or meaning. His words are not merely the symbols which record what he has discovered about life, they are the tools he uses to explore his world and mine its meaning.

V Commitment

The creative writer is a builder. He tries to make something out of the words he has used to discover life. He creates a meaning through what he says, and by doing so he reveals himself. This is not so much self-expression as self-exposure—and perhaps self-creation.

VI Detachment

After the creative writer has built something he forces himself to stand back and examine it. His toughest critic is his own cruel eye, for he is capable of the terrible double vision, seeing both what he meant and what he did. Through his detachment and cold self-examination he is able to mobilize his craft so he can move forward to discover new meanings and more effective forms.

VII Effectiveness

The creative writer's final test is communication. One writer will always write another writer, "Does it work?" What he means by that is, does it stand up after he has walked away, does it communicate to the reader not only the information, but also the feeling? The creative writer has to be practical and tough, always discounting intentions and demanding results.

• • •

If we accept these seven elements or stages of creative writing then we must face their implications for our teaching. Through them all runs the theme of individualization. A creative voice is a single voice, a recognizable voice which is different from the voices around it. It is unexpected, one of the finest surprises of life. And this single voice we call creative comes in its own time, in its own way, at its own pace.

The class cannot be creative, the individual can. There is no norm, no level by class, grade, age, sex, or race for creativity. The very idea of creativity implies the personal, the private, the individual and rejects the herd, mass or group. The creative teacher will teach by responding to each student as a person who deserves a personal reaction; he will not see himself as the teacher of the third grade but as the teacher of 27 third graders.

The teacher whose students achieve creative writing will allow plenty of time for pre-writing—awareness, caring, incubation. He will spend weeks and perhaps months with some of his students encouraging—and demonstrating—openness, honesty, the respect for the specific, concern, imagination. He will allow time for his students to perceive and for their subconscious to deal with what they have perceived.

The creative writing teacher will also allow time for writing, the production of the many drafts, the essential failures through which the student will find his own subject. Writing is discovery and commitment. By writing, the student discovers his questions and his answers. He uses words to explore his world and to create his world.

And finally, the teacher whose students write creatively encourages detachment. He shows them the necessity of standing back so that they can see the difference between what they wanted to do and what they have done, between what they have done and what they can do. The teacher encourages rewriting.

This is the cycle of craft—prewriting, writing, and rewriting. The student passes through it again and again, until he is finally ready for publication, where he finds out his effectiveness. When his peers and his teacher read the work he has chosen as his best, he discovers if it stands up, if it works, if it communicates, if he has built a meaning.

If the teacher is to encourage his students to pass through the cycle of craft and the final testing of publication at their own pace, he will discover that there are few chances for him to stand before the class and preach. He doesn't tell and he doesn't assign. He doesn't correct, he reads. He doesn't initiate, he reacts. He confers. He prods, and pulls, and goads, and praises. He is a coach.

If he wants his students to be open with him, then he will discover that he has to be open with his students. And if the teacher of writing is both open and courageous, then he has an opportunity which is almost unique in education. He can enter into the learning process with his students. No one ever learns to write, not Shakespeare, not Mailer, not Miss Mudget in the 5th Grade. The problem of finding something to say which is worth saying, and then saying it, is a problem which is ever new. And the teacher who shares his own struggles with his class will find that he has entered into an exciting and productive relationship with his students. He will not be a teacher, he will be a senior learner, what a teacher ought to be. And it's just possible that the teacher and the students who experience writing together may be creative.

It only seems a few years since the following article was published, but I'm afraid now that we teach composition in an age of conformity. Perhaps, if we're lucky, the pendulum will swing back.

20

Finding Your Own Voice

Teaching Composition in an Age of Dissent

Student power is no longer an issue, it is a fact. The war is being won—or lost—depending on your viewpoint, and one of the major weapons in the war is rhetoric that is crude, vigorous, usually uninformed, frequently obscene, and often threatening.

Most of us wonder what this educational revolution means for the composition teacher, who has often seen himself the principal defender of good taste, an evangelist of tradition, an heroic voice speaking up for order. Is our cause lost in an Age of Mailer?

No, but the implications of the student revolt for English Departments are clear. We are freed from an obligation to teach etiquette and forced to design a curriculum which trains students to accept the responsibilities of free speech through the experience of writing—the most disciplined form of thinking—and publication—the most revealing act of the intellectual life.

I do not speak from an isolated position. I teach in conference, close to my students. I am adviser to the college newspaper, and I suppose I am one of the New Left's enemy liberals, for I've been confronted, polarized, perhaps even co-opted. I am not over thirty; I'm over forty, and I feel it. I do get discouraged, mostly because the students have had no freedom, and when they find their own voice it has not been tempered by experience.

It is ironic that a nation built by teen-age pioneers, sea captains in their twenties, and statesmen in their early thirties has created a teacher-centered educational system which keeps most of its students in a state of permanent adolescence through, and sometimes beyond, the awarding of the Ph.D. Too often our students have not been allowed to speak, and when they have spoken no one has listened, and when we have listened we have not allowed the freedom of action which encourages responsibility.

Published in *College Composition and Communication,* May, 1969.

Our students need to discover, before graduation, that freedom is the greatest tyrant of all. Too often the composition teacher not only denies his students freedom, he even goes further and performs the key writing tasks for his students. He gives an assignment; he lists sources; he dictates the form; and, by irresponsibly conscientious correcting, he actually revises his students' papers. Is it not surprising that the student does not learn to write when the teacher, with destructive virtue, has done most of his student's writing?

The times indeed are revolutionary, cleansingly so. And they uniquely offer the composition teacher the opportunity to play a pioneer role in constructing an educational system which removes students' responsibilities from the teacher and places them firmly on the student.

Democracy is forged out of a responsible Babel, and the mature English teacher welcomes a diversity of contradictory voices, each student speaking of his own concerns in his own way. There is no single standard, no one way to think or to write, and we must not give our students the illusion there is. We must glory in contradiction and confusion, the human cacophony. Graham Greene has asked, "Isn't disloyalty as much the writer's virtue as loyalty is the soldier's?" Each writing teacher should be a revolutionary, doubting, questioning, challenging, and above all, encouraging his students to be individuals. He creates a constructive chaos which will allow the students to achieve effective communication.

The Four Responsibilities of the Student

The writing course is student-centered, but this does not imply a lack of standards or a casual permissiveness. Just the opposite. It places the obligation to learn on the student. It gives him four fundamental freedoms which he will discover are also responsibilities.

The Student's First Responsibility

The teacher should show the student how writers find their subjects. But the student must find his own subject. The teacher cannot see the student's world with the student's eyes and evaluate it with the student's mind. Every time the teacher gives an assignment he cheats the student, since each step in the writing process—form, style, tone, effectiveness—stems from what the student has to say.

The student may be shown how to perceive, but he has to do his own perceiving. The writing course is a tough course, perhaps the toughest the student will face, for he is made to look at his world and to react to it, honestly, critically, specifically, personally. If the student writer has nothing to say, he is a mute animal, uncritical, unspeaking, and he must realize it. It is the student's responsibility to find his own subject.

The Student's Second Responsibility

The student should also document his own subject so that he will build, in Lucile Vaughan Payne's words, "an informed opinion." The sturdy fact, the relevant detail, the esthetic insight, the revealing incident are the raw materials which he must collect to construct a piece of writing which supports his subject and convinces his reader.

Creativity is a tough business, and it all starts with a solid inventory of specifics. The student must either find the concrete details which he can arrange into a pattern of significance, or he can perceive a generalization and then nail it down with evidence. The poet is the most specific writer, the most accurate marksman, catching meanings on the wing. The novelist, the lawyer, the dramatist, the executive, the scientist, all depend on illuminating, revealing, relevant details as they write.

We can show our students how to search, but they must mine the nuggets of information themselves and refine the images or the facts which communicate meaning with authority, the smells and the sounds which give immediacy, the citations and statistics which persuade.

The search for information should not merely be autobiographical in a limited sense. The student does learn from the street corner, but he also learns from books. The coed who has worked as a waitress may be handed Orwell's *Down and Out in Paris and London,* or sent to an article on restaurant mangagement. The intellectual process does not mean just reading; it certainly does not mean just feeling.

Content always comes before form, and the student should begin to discover that the vigor of writing doesn't come so much from the graceful stroke of his pen as from the incisive bite of his intellect.

The Student's Third Responsibility

The act of writing is incomplete without a reader, but it is not the teacher's job to be a receptive audience of dull writing or force others to listen when nothing is being said. It is the student's responsibility to earn an audience, winning respect for what he has on the page.

The teacher of writing will break the class up so that individual students exchange papers. He will have his class read each other's papers in small groups. He will be an audience himself in conference. He will have his students write for the class, and perhaps write outside of the class.

No group is more peer-conscious than a covey of college professors. We should expect no less of our students. We learn as our publications are evaluated by our peers, the equals we respect. Our students will teach each other and learn from the same process. Often a student will understand another student's problem and its solution better than the instructor, for the student is working on the same level. It is the student's job to try to learn and to be a constructively critical audience so his classmates will learn.

The Student's Fourth Responsibility

I teach a course called Expository Writing, and students pre-register in May to exposit in October, when they may need to lyric, report, narrate and not exposit at all. The writer cannot predict the form in which he will express himself months in advance. When he sits down knowing his subject, knowing his audience, he may write narrative, poetry, argument, critical analysis, even exposition. During any writing course the student should practice many forms, each appropriate to what he has to say.

Perhaps, at times, it is appropriate for those who are interested in a particular form to sit down together. But there is something corrupt in forcing this, for the writer first has to have something to say to an audience before he can choose his form. He cannot choose the form until he knows the audience, knows the quantity and the quality of his evidence, knows his subject. You don't buy a wedding dress and then look for a wife. And yet I, too, fall into the pattern of asking my students to write description when they have nothing to describe, editorials when they have no opinions, reportage when they have nothing to report.

I am always tempted to return to this teaching method, dictating the form and, therefore, the content, for it is neat and comforting to the teacher. I know what I am doing, and the fact that it may not be relevant seems a lesser burden than doubt. Ultimately, however, I cheat the student, and somehow I must make him see that there are many forms which he is capable of choosing. Each artistic form is inherent, arising out of the artistic situation. It is third down and four; you are behind 17 to 14; the defensive team has over shifted to the left—the writer processes as much information as the quarterback, or more, and then chooses his form. It arises out of what he has to say and to whom he wishes to say it. And the choice of form belongs to him.

In this age of dissent the student must be given four freedoms—the freedom to find his own subject, to find his own evidence, to find his own audience, and to find his own form. These freedoms are his opportunity and his obligation.

The Four Responsibilities of the Teacher

The teacher who has the courage to place the student's responsibilities on the student's shoulders finds himself in a frightening position. He can not take the aggressive role of pouring information into the students' heads; he must wait for them to write so that he can react.

Students are promoted and rewarded in our educational system for their ability to follow directons; taking orders, not taking the initiative, is the way to get into college. When the teacher forces a responsible role on his students they will at first resent and distrust the teacher—he is not doing his job—and they will be frightened—what does teacher want? But the professor should not compound the felonies of the past. If he is patient, at first a few, and then a majority, of his students will accept and even enjoy their freedom and its attendant responsibility to learn by primarily teaching themselves.

The Teacher's First Responsibility

The teacher's primary responsibility is to create a psychological and physical environment in which the student can fulfill his responsibilities.

At the University of New Hampshire we have created a writing laboratory with twenty-four typewriters around the walls and a hollow square of movable tables which can be adapated to group activity. There is good lighting and good soundproofing, so that many people can work and talk and criticize simultaneously. There is a 40-foot-long wall of corkboard for articles on writing. An office opens off the laboratory where there are four file cabinets full of materials which can be given to the students during conference, a library on writing, an unabridged dictionary, and comfortable chairs where the student and the teacher can sit side by side to examine a paper. Most important, there is a dittoed sheet on the door with at least 44 fifteen-minute conference slots a week.

The psychological implications of this writing laboratory are more important than the physical setting, and they can be duplicated in the ordinary classroom. The emphasis in the writing course is on conferences which are held at the student's initiative. Teaching is done individually or around a table. The writing lab dramatizes the intellectual act of writing. Everything is designed to help the individual student find his own way to satisfy the essential discipline of the course.

The Teacher's Second Responsibility

Once the teacher has created an environment in which the student can write, then he must enforce the deadline. The student must write frequently, and probably to a minimum daily deadline, an artificial necessity. A paper a day, or five pages a week, or ten pages every two weeks. I've not had much success with a class deadline much beyond that. Formal outlines, carefully done notes, sloppy first-draft, total revisions—all count toward the number of pages.

Once students understand the system and are convinced of the need of the deadline, they will experience the process of writing and welcome the discipline of frequent papers. They will learn to write by writing. Most students who come to me with critical writing problems have never had an intensive writing experience, while the students who enter the course writing well have passed through a course where they wrote and wrote and wrote. The teacher cannot shirk his responbility to force the student to write. He must create artificial pressure which makes the student commit himself on paper again and again and again.

The Teacher's Third Responsibility

The writing teacher has to stop trying to create a world in which success for the majority day by day is the norm. He has to cultivate a climate of failure. The writer fails all the time, but he fails to succeed. He learns to shape the failure of his drafts into the successes of his final copy.

Grades, of course, are ridiculous during the writing course. They are much more than irrelevant, they do positive harm. An "A" deludes a student into thinking an early draft is final copy, while an ''F'' convinces another student that there is no hope. The teachers I know who have experimented with eliminating grades on individual pieces of writing never return to conventional grading. The productivity and the quality of student writing increases when grades are left off each paper. Of course, when the time comes for a final standard, it is easy enough to evaluate papers chosen by the students at the end of the course.

The Teacher's Fourth Responsibility

The teacher is a diagnostician. Ideally, the teacher reads only those papers on which the student is having problems. He knows those papers because his students select them from their folder in conference. He does not write long, careful, but easily misinterpreted comments on papers most of the time. He listens to the student in conference, reads the papers selected by the student, listens to the student's own diagnosis of his writing problems, confirms it or proposes an alternate diagnosis, listens to the student as he proposes his own solutions, and possibly suggests alternate treatments.

The experienced composition teacher does not see all writing problems —spelling and structure, and lack of subject matter—of equal importance. He encourages the student to see that on most pieces of writing there is one fundamental problem which must be dealt with before the next problem can be spotted, and then solved. For example, an incoherent paper will be ungrammatical; once the logic of the writing is developed, grammatical problems tend to disappear.

The effective teacher rarely corrects a paper. That's too easy for him. Sometimes he will edit a paragraph or a page, particularly on a good paper, to show how it may be shaped into a still better paper, but this must be done with discretion. The teacher who corrects an entire paper is doing the student's job of editing. He is cheating the student of the opportunity to learn, for ultimately the student must be able to diagnose and treat his own problems when he has escaped the protective custody of his writing teacher.

The Responsibility Shared by Teacher and Student

The central act of the writing course is publication. This is the crucible where the student is tested, tried and taught. And the teacher, as well as the student, must publish and share criticism from careful readers.

The teacher, by writing with his students and by failing with them, will not lose but earn their respect. He will have the enviable opportunity to share the experience of learning with his students. Together they can establish an environment of exploration and discovery.

Publication within the classroom may be performed with ditto, xerox, carbon paper, overhead projector, wall display, or merely student folders open to all members of the class. The means are not important; the ends are. The writer must face his audience. He must hear the contradictory counsel of his readers, so that he learns when to ignore his teacher and his peers, listening to himself after evaluating what has been said about his writing and considering what he can do to make it work.

Slowly, painfully, the student will discover he can achieve an audience. If he has something to say, if he says it honestly, if his opinions are informed, if he brings order to chaos, if he entertains, if he is able to give the reader information or an esthetic experience, he will be read.

The free speech movement may start with dirty words, but a cliché is a cliché, and if the audience is not shocked or frightened by short transitive verbs, then the student can go on to say what he has to say. He will reveal, as we all do, our lack of information, our naivete, our clumsiness, our dishonesties. He will experience criticism, failure, and enough success—those nice small moments of completion—to give him courage, in the right environment, to face the agonies of exposure on the printed page and to learn from it.

The teacher of composition should welcome an age of dissent. He should glory in diversity, and he should discover that by giving his students freedom they will accept responsibility. Perhaps in this age when students are using their voices to attack and transform the educational establishment, the teacher of composition may return to his important educational role when rhetoric—the art of effective and responsible argument—was the foundation of a classical education.

The greatest problem we have in school may well be a lack of faith. I know that that's my greatest problem as a writer. I fail to have faith in myself. If we have faith in ourselves as writers—if we have heard our own voices—then we can have faith in our students—and hear their voices. Most of us who are experienced teachers of writing have our faith rewarded. We hear our students' voices and, when we hear them, they begin to hear each other and themselves. I know they can write, and I project that confidence on my students. I expect them to write well, and they do.

21
Our Students Will Write - If We Let Them

Our students want to write—but not what we want them to write.

Our students want to write of death and love and hate and fear and loyalty and disloyalty; they want to write the themes of literature in those forms—poetry, narrative, drama—which have survived the centuries. They want to write literature, and we assign them papers of literary analysis, comparison and contrast, argumentation based on subjects on which they are not informed and for which they have no concern.

English teachers may believe in the writing crisis, but writing teachers know that even in a multi-media electronic, passive spectator age everyone seems to want to write. The history teacher, the chemistry teacher, the coach, even fellow English teachers are closet writers. Principals, superintendents, schoolboard members, taxpayers are likely to press, shyly but firmly, a bulky manuscript into the writing teacher's hand. Others may be surprised that when the Russian poet, Joseph Brodsky, was being questioned by the KGB, his interrogator submitted his own manuscripts for Brodsky's criticism. Writing teachers aren't surprised.

Research supports the impression that everyone wants to write. Carol Chomsky, and others, have shown that children want to write before they want to read. Donald Graves' research indicates that the less writing assigned, the more produced. At the University of New Hampshire we continue to offer more and more sections of writing courses, and we can not satisfy the demand. Kenneth Koch is doing exciting work in nursing homes with writers who are

Published in *North Carolina English Teacher,* Fall, 1977.

70, 80, 90, 100 years old. The hunger to write survives as long as the breath to live.

Workshops on the teaching of writing should begin with the teachers writing. I run many such workshops, and the teachers write as their students should on subjects of their own choice in forms appropriate to the evolving subject. They never choose literary analysis, argumentation, or any of the forms usually called expository. They write description and narration, embryonic poems and stories. They are astonished and impressed at what they write and at what their colleagues write. Writing in a hurry, on demand, under impossible conditions, they produce moving and exciting writing which deals with the major themes of loss and birth and discovery and failure and survival. Their voices are vigorous, sad, angry, nostalgic, amused, diverse and individual.

These are the same voices I hear from Grade Three through post-doctoral students, but I didn't see the full import of what I observed until Richard Barbieri, head of the English Department at Milton Academy, told me a student of his charged that they had to write essays of literary analysis while they read poetry and fiction, "because you don't want our reading to be boring, you just want our writing to be boring."

We all know that the essay can be exciting, but we also know that the essay topics assigned in class to test knowledge of literature rarely produce exciting or even interesting writing.

I have begun to realize I must reconsider the new emphasis on expository writing in our schools, especially with beginning students, and reconsider our attitude towards creative writing. That is a term I hate. All writers I know resent it. The connotation of creative writing is frivolous writing, decorative writing, writing that is all style and no content, writing that is superficial, avocational, sometimes therapeutic, most times trivial.

Unfortunately, we can all point to creative writing classes in which there is more therapy than writing, a patronizing approval of all efforts, an irresponsible lack of standards. These "like wow, man, that's like real, I mean, wow" creative therapy units have turned many of us away from a proper examination of what happens when creative writing classes are taught by professional writing teachers.

In those classes the students and teacher alike examine, through writing, the most important issues in their lives, and they do it through the forms we call literary—poetry, fiction, drama, non-fiction.

As English teachers we should all be delighted that creative writing courses are popular and accept the people who teach them as equals in our profession. We usually, however, do not. We do not trust writers although we admire their work when they are dead. We do not believe that our students are capable of attempting literature.

We should see that their desire to write proves the vitality and importance of literature and literature-making in each generation, that language is central to the human experience, not just as a communications skill but as the best way to recall and understand experience. We tell our students the unexamined life is not worth living, yet we seldom allow those students to examine their lives firsthand through what is termed creative writing.

It is time that we, as a profession, not only support the reading of literature but the making of literature; that we encourage our students to write what they want to write and realize that what they want to write is more intellectually demanding, more linguistically challenging, more rhetorically difficult than the writing we usually require in the English class.

The biggest problem in the teaching of writing is ourselves. We do not encourage, allow, or respond to our students' desire to write. We do not believe that our students can write anything worth reading, and they prove our prediction. Conditions will not improve until we realize that what we face is a teacher problem, not a student problem.

When I was in junior high school the public address system announced that piano lessons would be available, and interested students should report to the cafeteria. We had a piano at home, and I had been fascinated by it, but no one in the family could even play chopsticks, and I was not allowed to touch it. I reported to the cafeteria for piano lessons. They cost 25¢ a week in those days of the Depression, but I could earn that after school. At last I would be able to make music.

I didn't know that there was a new method of teaching piano. When I reported for my first lesson there was a single piano on the stage, and 50 of us ($12.50 worth) assigned to separate places at cafeteria tables. We were each given our own cardboard keyboard, which we unfolded on command. The teacher played on the stage and we drummed our fingers against the cardboard keyboard in awkward imitation.

We were told this new method had been developed by experts. We were commanded to shut any pianos we had at home and lock them. We would learn to play before we were allowed to play. Week after week I drummed by fingers against my cardboard keyboard, but I could hear no music. Then I missed one day of practice, and then another, one lesson and then another. I still do not play the piano.

I fear that the teaching of writing in our schools has similarities, and the back-to-the-basics emphasis on expository writing, on workbooks, on rhetorical models, on sentence combining, forces our students to play cardboard keyboards. They can not hear their voices any more than I could hear music from the silent exercises I was forced to practice; they are not allowed to use their own language to discover their own meaning in their own existence.

There are many important reasons to consider taking what is usually tolerated, at best, in the elective creative writing course and placing it at the center of the writing curriculum. Some of them are:

- Writing about individual human experience motivates both the gifted and those we often consider disadvantaged. In fact, we may find that the disadvantaged aren't in terms of experiences which can be explored through writing. Students who are not motivated by our lectures on the need for writing skills—they know the need does not exist in the lives they expect to live—still share the human hunger to record and examine experience. Students who are bored with papers of literary analysis or even incapable of writing such a paper at this stage in their development may be able to write extraordinary papers based on first-person experience.

- Students discover, through creative writing, that they have a voice, they have a way of looking at their own life through their own language. They discover and learn to respect their own individuality.
- Creative writing extends experience and orders it. Through writing, the student increases his or her awareness of the world, and then works to order that awareness.
- As students follow language towards meaning they extend and stretch their linguistic skills.
- The experience-centered, doing nature of the writing curriculum will reach many students who are not comfortable with the analytical, passive-receptive nature of the typical academic curriculum.
- Students, through writing, discover the satisfaction of making. They think writing is an art and discover it is a craft.
- Creative writing gives students a new insight to literature. The study of literature is no longer entirely a spectator sport, but an activity which they can experience and appreciate.
- The creative writing class may be the place where some students learn to read. Test results in many community colleges and other colleges of the second chance show that many students who test as not being able to read are also the best writers.They are able to read their own words and to perform the complex, evaluative techniques essential to revision. They learn to read by writing.
- Students and teachers of creative writing rediscover the fun of writing. Art is, at the center, play, and perhaps that is the reason it is so little tolerated in the school. If it is fun can it be learning? Yes.
- Finally, we should teach creative writing because it is more intellectually demanding than the study of literature or language as they are usually taught in the English class. This runs directly counter to the stereotype believed by most English teachers. It is easier to complete a workbook on grammar, easier to tell the teacher what the teacher wants to know about a story than it is to use language to make meaning out of experience. The writing course is a thinking course, and it should be central to the curriculum in any school.

If we face up to this responsibility to get back to the real basics in writing and allow our students the opportunity to use language meaningfully to explore experience, then we must face the feeling of inadequacy shared by almost all English teachers. We teach language and literature because that is what we have been trained to teach. We do not teach writing because few English teachers have ever had a course in writing or in the methods of teaching writing.

Fortunately the teaching of writing is within the reach of every English teacher. The teacher can teach himself or herself to teach writing by attempting an experimental curriculum based on three simple principles:

1. *Teach process not product.* The traditional English class appropriately deals with a product—finished writing. The writing class deals with unfinished writing, writing that is in the process of discovering meaning. Students must have the time to pass through the same stages of prewriting, writing, rewriting and editing which writers have to pass through to achieve the products we examine in other parts of the English curriculum.

   Classes in which we give assignments and grade first drafts produce the kind of writing we deplore. We must allow students to find their own subjects, using their own language to discover meaning in experience.
2. *Write yourself.* The writing teacher prepares for the writing class by using his or her own language to examine and share experience. The teacher understands the writing process because the teacher experiences it.
3. *Listen to your students.* The center of the writing course is the conference in which the student evaluates the draft and the teacher responds to that evaluation. Students who are experiencing the process understand it better than we can. They know what is going well, what isn't going well, and they can, with our coaching, see how to improve their writing—to move closer to their meaning.

It sounds simple, and it is. It takes an act of courage and an act of faith. We have to commit ourselves to letting our students take the initiative in the writing course. Their writing is the text of the course, and we have to respond to that. To do so we have to have the courage to wait and, possibly, to fail. At the same time we have to have faith that our students have something to say, that they have a language and a life, and that their language and their life can work against each other to ignite meaning.

It is significant that these acts of courage and faith correspond directly to the acts of courage and faith demanded of each writer, students or professional, when he or she faces a new draft. We have to have the courage to commit ourselves to the page, to reveal ourselves, to fail. And we have to have faith that the act of commitment and revelation may be worthwhile, may produce meaning.

If we have this courage and this faith we will discover that our students can write, and that they will write, and that we will be eager to read what they have written. There will be no writing crises in our classroom. There will be the excitement of students finding voices and the voices producing writing which is memorable and meaningful. Our students will write—if we let them.

At the University of New Hampshire in our freshman English course, from which no student is exempted, as well as in our sophomore writing course and in most of our advanced writing courses, we have weekly conferences. I estimated that last year we had more than 64,000 writing conferences in Hamilton Smith Hall.

This concentration on teaching writing one-on-one has led to a great deal of experimentation with conference techniques. The following four articles reflect some of my own evolving concerns with the writing conference. Incidentally, in my own case, I feel that at least 85% of the teaching—or learning—takes place in the writing conference, not in the writing workshop or classroom, and in recent years my workshops have become an extension of the writing conference.

22
What Can You Say Besides Awk?

That stagefright moment of anticipation and apprehension all good teachers feel before each new term does not hit the writing teacher as he walks into his first class. His anxiety is delayed. He suffers when he sits down to read his first batch of student papers. What will they say? What will he say? What is there to say beside "awk"?

He can choose one of three roles. He can play *judge*—the defender of the institution. He will evaluate the papers and penalize any student who breaks the law. To the judge, all rules are absolute, misdemeanors as well as felonies must be identified and the perpetrator punished. Sentence fragment: pay a fine. Clumsy paragraph: go to the workhouse.

This is a comfortable role for the teacher—and for many students. The superficial takes precedence over the important, and there is no doubt where anyone stands. There is the comforting illusion of simple, clear, impersonal standards for writing. There are also, however, a couple of problems. The students serve their sentence with the judge and then go on breaking rules. And the few of them who become writers find there aren't many rules anyway. Language lives, evolves; rules are not what writers do, but what writers have done.

Another role the writing teacher can adopt is that of *Moses.* He is the bearer of great truths. He believes that there is a normal academic content to the writing course, and he feels he must deliver an absolute rhetoric written on

Published in *California English Journal,* December, 1973.

tablets from on high to the young. He applies form when there is not yet content.

Moses's students may not yet have anything to say—at least nothing Moses thinks worth saying—but they produce assigned papers, mass exercises in form. They write description, argument, any form the teacher wants, on command. The students have form but no subject, and since they do not see that form is the vehicle of meaning they learn little. Many of the students develop the misconception that how you say it is more important than what you say.

A third role is that of the *listener*. He waits, he reads, he listens. He is far less dramatic as a teacher, and he is far less sure of himself, for he has few strict laws to enforce and few great truths to thunder.

The listening writing teacher believes his students' papers are the content of the writing course. The students write the text as the term unfolds. He does not put content into his students, he draws out what is there. The responsive teacher has few preconceptions. When his students ask him, "What do you want?" he answers, "Surprise me." And he means it. And he is surprised. And notice what happens; students who do not write for the judge or for Moses, write for him.

The responsive, listening teacher builds his program on four assumptions:

1. *He respects the student's potential.* He sees his students—even in the primary grades—as experienced human beings who have had extensive contact with life and language. He realizes their principal problem is lack of self-respect—they do not think they have anything to say or the words with which to say it. He sees his job, first of all, to convince each individual student he has something worth saying and his own way of saying it.
2. *He sees writing as a process, not a product.* He understands each piece of writing is a draft, work in process which is always capable of improvement. The responsive teacher understands the stages of prewriting, writing, and rewriting. He doesn't force his students through these stages, but he uses his knowledge of them to allow his students to take the time they need as he coaches them through the evolution from idea to communication.
3. *He defers grades until the end of the term.* The other day I showed a student a book in which manuscript pages are reproduced. She said, "If Malamud's first draft is that bad, there's hope for me." Of course there is. Writers are not graded on their early drafts. If they were, most authors would flunk. Writers are evaluated when they have finished a piece of writing and submit their best work for evaluation by editors, and students should have the same right.
4. *He teaches individuals.* The experienced writing teacher knows the slow student may be intelligent and the fast student glib. He recognizes different writing tasks demand different working methods. He does not give class assignments, because writing is an individual act and

assignments rob the student of essential experience in finding his own subject, audience, and form. He doesn't correct papers; he tries to diagnose a key problem and suggest some of the alternate ways in which the student may solve them.

Well, what does the writing teacher do? How does he earn his money if he doesn't lecture, direct class assignments, and correct papers? He listens for voices.

What do you mean, listens for voices? He doesn't look for what he hopes will be there or ought to be there, instead he listens for what is there. He is ready for the unexpected, alert to a hint, a word, a tone, a fact, a shape, a subject, an attitude which will make him respond as a reader, a human being, not an English teacher.

As the responsive teacher listens to thousands of papers he will discover there are four clues to a student's writing potential. He scans the papers, waiting for these elements to appear where he least expects them. Rarely are they fully developed, and they often lie behind a dreadful tangle of syntax. But he knows when he spots a glimpse of one of these elements that he is meeting a potential writer and that he will be able to encourage him to write.

1. *Honesty.* Most rare. Most important. Nurture the student who speaks honestly of his world, who is direct, candid, accurate. There are few things as exciting as hearing the true word, the word which is precisely right, the word which reveals the form, entertains, explains, persuades. You mean that in a paper which is scrawled, misspelled and ungrammatical that you may respond to just one word? Yes.
2. *Subject.* The teacher looks for a subject on which the student may be an authority. Good writing is often writing which satisfies the reader's curiosity with authoritative knowledge. The student is an authority on many subjects—how to survive on his block, how to milk a goat, repair a motorcycle, ride a wave, perform a song, care for a grandmother—a dozen subjects, a hundred. And the teacher should make no judgment of which subject is worthy of the writer's attention. All subjects are, for the student must write from his own knowing and his own caring.
3. *Structure.* Admire students who can observe accurately and order their observations into meaning. Science students who think English isn't for them may be taught to write by building on their organizational ability far more easily than the student of verbal ability who can not order what he has to say. The poet, after all, does nothing less than bring order to chaos.
4. *Tone.* The student, in his writing, is speaking. The student with his own tone of voice rises off the page, perhaps in just a phrase, a sentence, a few words, but enough to reveal his whole attitude, his point of view, his tone of voice.

What do you do when you spot a touch of honesty, recognize that the student has a potential subject, sense a feeling for structure, hear an individual tone of voice? Praise him. Give your students earned praise, not patronizing pats on the head, but deserved portions of praise. Give them your respect for both what they have done and what they may do because of it.

All students learn best from a position of confidence. But this is especially true of those who are trying to learn the revealing act of writing. The student has to believe he has something to say before he can say it. The writing teacher's methods usually move from more to less as he gains experience. At first he heavily marks the paper, but after a while he realizes there is usually one central problem, and he tries to help the student identify it.

Then he begins to see that the problem often comes from the fact that the student hasn't developed his potential, so the teacher begins to identify the point of greatest potential. As he gains experience, the writing teacher realizes that many early drafts are really pre-drafts and do not need detailed written criticism. The student, for example, who has no subject has no paper. There is no reason to identify all the problems which arise when a writer is trying to write something about nothing.

Usually the writing teacher finds himself making fewer and finally no marks on the paper. He discovers he teaches most effectively in conference, and finds that frequent, short conferences are most effective. He begins to turn the conference over to the student, asking the student, first of all, about his paper—what was its greatest strength? what is its greatest weakness? what does he intend to do with it?—drawing out of the student what he knows. Then his students really begin to learn.

In teaching writing, as in creating art, less is usually more. The teacher teaches less in the formal sense as he encourages his students to criticize and improve their own papers in their own way. Every teacher of writing wants to deal with the paper rather than the person who wrote it. We are at our best when we have a piece of work which is nearly finished and which may be helped by some specific suggestions. But in the beginning that rarely happens. There are few papers worthy of such careful consideration. We have to deal with the person first. The writing teacher has to get to know the student—he has to listen.

Let's eavesdrop on some of the conference comments of experienced writing teachers at the beginning of the year. Remember that conferences are quick, frequent, and informal. They may take place in the corridor, on the playground, or during one of the breaks during the normal school day.

"Hey, I couldn't believe that one-handed catch."

"I hear you're a horse nut. Do you know Marguerite Henry's books?"

"I hear you're taking care of the family while your mother's in the hospital. Are you going to bring me a sample of your cooking?"

"Mr. Handley showed me those pictures of yours. You've got a good eye."

"You look like a real pro at the supermarket. How many hours a week do you work?"

Is this teaching English? Are these appropriate comments for a teacher? Is this professional behavior? Have these comments got anything to do with writing? Yes. Good writing is built on a foundation of self-respect. The writer is one who knows something someone else needs to know. When a student writes papers that have no subject, it won't help to say "awk." Most of the time the student knows only too well it is awk. What the teacher has to do is to establish a relationship in which the student discovers he is an individual who has something worthwhile saying. Gradually the teacher will be trying to draw subject matter out of his students to make them see the potential raw material which they think is obvious. He doesn't assign the student to use this material, but he shows the student that he may have a potential subject.

"I see you're always breaking everybody up in the lunchroom. Did you ever try to write humor?"

"I'd be interested, and I know others would, if you could tell us how you develop pictures."

"One of the ways to get those playground rules changed would be to write a petition to the principal."

"I don't know anybody else in the class who's been down in a submarine. What's it feel like: How cramped are you?"

"Did you ever try to write words for those songs of yours?"

Once a student begins to find his subject and limit it, the writing teacher can move closer to the student's page and deal with questions of form and development.

The effective teacher must be sure not to dictate a repsonse. He must try to be tentative, make only suggestions to help the student realize that there are constant choices which the writer has to make for himself.

"What do you think of this paper? It seems to me it ought to be either shorter or longer."

"I think this is a pretty good paper, but I wonder what would happen if you'd try it in the third person, made it a story."

"I've never been in an earthquake. This is exciting but I need a lot more. What did you hear? What did you feel like? What did people do? I can't wait to read another draft."

"If you haven't read this aloud, try it. You'll see where your voice is strong and where it falters. You've got a good ear, use it."

"I'm just getting a whiff of what you have to say. You've whetted my appetite, now I want some specifics."

As the year goes on, the teacher will have more and more papers which are worthy of line-by-line examination. Here the student can discover the fun of making the craftsman's choice. How are these choices made? By rule? No, by meaning. Each word, each phrase, each construction, each bit of information is chosen for its ability to communicate truth to the reader. The teacher may make a few suggestions, but they are always tentative. It is the writer's meaning, not the teacher's.

Many teachers believe that they need a special, professional language to be an effective critic. This simply isn't true. The language the teacher-editor uses should be simple, his comments should force the student to reconsider what he has said in terms of what he meant to say, not in terms of a linguistic or rhetorical tradition.

"It seems to me this may need a little work in here. Perhaps these short sentences jounce the reader along too fast. Maybe if you could hook them together and slow things down it would help."

"This is an exciting piece of writing, but I'm pretty dumb about motorcycles. I've underlined the words I don't understand. You've either got to use simpler words or tell the reader what they mean."

"Read this aloud. . . . Now then, I don't think those words sound like you. What do you think?"

"This is an exciting story, but all your verbs are kind of blah. Why don't you see if you can make your verbs active, simple, direct? If it ruins the story blame me."

"You've got an awful lot to tell me, but it's like a freeway wreck. Everything is run on into the thing ahead of it. I wonder what would happen if you'd slowed down and told me one thing at a time?"

"I never won any spelling bees, but when you spell like this that's all the reader sees. He just doesn't listen to what you have to say, and what you have to say is important."

These are just a few of the things you can say beside "awk." How you say them will depend on your personality and the personality of your students. If you do make comments like these, however, you will draw out of your students much better writing than you ever thought possible. And when you get a good piece of writing you'll be able to publish it before the class on ditto, with an overhead projector, by posting on the board—whatever method you have available.

When you publish good writing you're liable to start an epidemic, for honest, effective writing is contagious. Students respond to the excitement of hearing individual human voices speaking directly of what they know. They will recognize that they have something to say and a voice with which to say it.

Can this miracle be guaranteed? Yes, without qualification, not because what the experienced writing teacher knows, but because of what your student has within him. The teacher of writing doesn't put in, he draws out. Good writing is within your student, and you'll hear it if you listen—and don't scrawl "awk."

23
The Listening Eye
Reflections on the Writing Conference

It was dark when I arrived at my office this winter morning, and it is dark again as I wait for my last writing student to step out of the shadows in the corridor for my last conference. I am tired, but it is a good tired, for my students have generated energy as well as absorbed it. I've learned something of what it is to be a childhood diabetic, to raise oxen, to work across from your father at 115 degrees in a steel-drum factory, to be a welfare mother with three children, to build a bluebird trail, to cruise the disco scene, to be a teen-age alcoholic, to salvage World War II wreckage under the Atlantic, to teach invented spelling to first graders, to bring your father home to die of cancer. I have been instructed in other lives, heard the voices of my students they had not heard before, shared their satisfaction in solving the problems of writing with clarity and grace. I sit quietly in the late afternoon waiting to hear what Andrea, my next student, will say about what she accomplished on her last draft and what she intends on her next draft.

It is nine weeks into the course and I know Andrea well. She will arrive in a confusion of scarves, sweaters and canvas bags, and then produce a clipboard from which she will precisely read exactly what she has done and exactly what she will do. I am an observer of her own learning, and I am eager to hear what she will tell me.

I am surprised at this eagerness. I am embedded in tenure, undeniably middle-aged, one of the gray, fading professors I feared I would become, but still have not felt the bitterness I saw in many of my own professors and see in some of my colleagues. I wonder if I've missed something important, if I'm becoming one of those aging juveniles who bound across the campus from concert to lecture, pleasantly silly.

There must be something wrong with a fifty-four-year-old man who is looking forward to his thirty-fifth conference of the day. It is twelve years since I really started teaching by conference. I average seventy-five conferences a week, thirty weeks a year, then there's summer teaching and workshop teaching of teachers. I've probably held far more than 30,000 writing conferences, and I am still fascinated by this strange, exposed kind of teaching, one on one.

It doesn't seem possible to be an English teacher without the anxiety that I will be exposed by my colleagues. They will find out how little I do; my students will expose me to them; the English Department will line up in military formation in front of Hamilton Smith Hall and, after the buttons are cut off my Pendleton shirt, my university library card will be torn once across each way and let flutter to the ground.

Published in *College English,* September, 1979.

The other day I found myself confessing to a friend, "Each year I teach less and less, and my students seem to learn more. I guess what I've learned to do is to stay out of their way and not to interfere with their learning."

I can still remember my shock years ago when I was summoned by a secretary from my classroom during a writing workshop. I had labored hard but provoked little discussion. I was angry at the lack of student involvement and I was angry at the summons to the department office. I stomped back to the classroom and was almost in my chair before I realized the classroom was full of talk about the student papers. My students were not even aware I had returned. I moved back out to the corridor, feeling rejected, and let the class teach itself.

Of course, that doesn't always happen, and you have to establish the climate, the structure, the attitude. I know all that, and yet...

I used to mark up every student paper diligently. How much I hoped my colleagues would see how carefully I marked up student papers. I alone held the bridge against the pagan hordes. No one escaped the blow of my "awk." And then one Sunday afternoon a devil bounded to the arm of my chair. I started giving purposefully bad counsel on my students' papers to see what would happen. "Do this backward," "add adjectives and adverbs," "be general and abstract," "edit with a purple pencil," "you don't mean black you mean white." Not one student questioned my comments.

I was frightened my students would pay so much attention to me. They took me far more seriously than I took myself. I remembered a friend in advertising told me about a head copywriter who accepted a piece of work from his staff and held it overnight without reading it. The next day he called in the staff and growled, "Is this the best you can do?"

They hurried to explain that if they had more time they could have done better. He gave them more time. And when they met the new deadline, he held their copy again without reading it, and called them together again and said, "Is *this* the best you can do?"

Again they said if only they had more time, they could... He gave them a new deadline. Again he held their draft without reading. Again he gave it back to them. Now they were angry. They said, yes, it was best they could do and he answered, "I'll read it."

I gave my students back their papers, unmarked, and said, make them better. And they did. That isn't exactly the way I teach now, not quite, but I did learn something about teaching writing.

In another two-semester writing course I gave 220 hours of lecture during the year. My teaching evaluations were good; students signed up to take this course in advance. Apparently I was well-prepared, organized, entertaining. No one slept in my class, at least with their eyes shut, and they did well on the final exam. But that devil found me in late August working over my lecture notes and so, on the first day of class, I gave the same final exam I had given at the end of the year. My students did better before the 220 hours of lectures than my students had done afterwards. I began to learn something about teaching a non-content writing course, about under-teaching, about not teaching what my students already know.

The other day a graduate student who wanted to teach writing in a course I supervise indicated, "I have no time for non-directive teaching. I know what my students need to know. I know the problems they will have—and I teach them."

I was startled, for I do not know what my students will be able to do until they write without any instructions from me. But he had a good reputation, and I read his teaching evalutions. The students liked him, but there was a minor note of discomfort. "He does a good job of teaching, but I wish he would not just teach me what I already know" and "I wish he would listen better to what we need to know." But they liked him. They could understand what he wanted, and they could give it to him. I'm uncomfortable when my students are uncomfortable, but more uncomfortable when they are comfortable.

I teach the student not the paper but this doesn't mean I'm a "like wow" teacher. I am critical and I certainly can be directive but I listen before I speak. Most times my students make tough—sometimes too tough evaluations—of their work. I have to curb their too critical eye and help them see what works and what might work so they know how to read evolving writing so it will evolve into writing worth reading.

I think I've begun to learn the right questions to ask at the beginning of a writing conference.

"What did you learn from this piece of writing?"

"What do you intend to do in the next draft?"

"What surprised you in the draft?"

"Where is the piece of writing taking you?"

"What do you like best in the piece of writing?"

"What questions do you have of me?"

I feel as if I have been searching for years for the right questions, questions which would establish a tone of master and apprentice, no, the voice of a fellow craftsman having a conversation about a piece of work, writer to writer, neither praise nor criticism but questions which imply further drafts, questions which draw helpful comments out of the student writer.

And now that I have my questions, they quickly become unnecessary. My students ask these questions of themselves before they come to me. They have taken my conferences away from me. They come in and tell me what has gone well, what has gone wrong, and what they intend to do about it.

Some of them drive an hour or more for a conference that is over in fifteen minutes. It is pleasant and interesting to me, but don't they feel cheated? I'm embarrassed that they tell me what I would hope I would tell them, but probably not as well. My students assure me it is important for them to prepare themselves for the conference and to hear what I have to say.

"But I don't say anything," I confess. "You say it all."

They smile and nod as if I know better than that, but I don't.

What am I teaching? At first I answered in terms of form: argument, narrative, description. I never said comparison and contrast, but I was almost as bad as that. And then I grew to answering, "the process." "I teach the writing process." "I hope my students have the experience of the writing process." I hear my voice coming back from the empty rooms which have held teacher workshops.

That's true, but there's been a change recently. I'm really teaching my students to react to their own work in such a way that they write increasingly effective drafts. They write; they read what they've written; they talk to me about what they've read and what the reading has told them they should do. I nod and smile and put my feet up on the desk, or down on the floor, and listen and stand up when the conference runs too long. And I get paid for this?
stand up when the conference runs too long. And I get paid for this?

Of course, what my students are doing, if they've learned how to ask the right questions, is write oral rehearsal drafts in conference.They tell me what they are going to write in the next draft, and they hear their own voices telling me. I listen and they learn.

But I thought a teacher had to talk. I feel guilty when I do nothing but listen. I confess my fear that I'm too easy, that I have too low standards, to a colleague, Don Graves. He assures me I am a demanding teacher, for I see more in my students than they do—to their surprise, not mine.

I hear voices from my students they have never heard from themselves. I find they are authorities on subjects they think ordinary. I find that even my remedial students write like writers, putting down writing that doesn't quite make sense, reading it to see what sense there might be in it, trying to make sense of it, and—draft after draft—making sense of it. They follow language to see where it will lead them, and I follow them following language.

It is a matter of faith, faith that my students have something to say and a language in which to say it. Sometimes I lose that faith but if I regain it and do not interfere, my students do write and I begin to hear things that need saying said well.

This year, more than ever before, I realize I'm teaching my students what they've just learned.

They experiment, and when the experiment works I say, "See, look what happened." I put the experiment in the context of the writing process. They brainstorm, and I tell them that they've brainstormed. They write a discovery draft, and I point out that many writers have to do that. They revise, and then I teach them revision.

When I boxed I was a counterpuncher. And I guess that's what I'm doing now, circling my students, waiting, trying to shut up—it isn't easy—trying not to interfere with their learning, waiting until they've learned something so I can show them what they've learned. There is no text in my course until my students write. I have to study the new text they write each semester.

It isn't always an easy text to read. The student has to decode the writing teacher's text; the writing teacher has to decode the student's writing. The writing teacher has to read what hasn't been written yet. The writing teacher has the excitement of reading unfinished writing.

Those papers without my teacherly comments written on them haunt me. I can't escape the paranoia of my profession. Perhaps I should mark up their pages. There are misspellings, comma splices, sentence fragments (even if they are now sanctified as "English minor sentences.") Worse still, I get papers that have no subject, no focus, no structure, papers that are undeveloped and papers that are voiceless.

I am a professional writer—a hired pen who ghostwrites and edits—yet I do not know how to correct most student papers. How do I change the language when the student writer doesn't yet know what to say? How do I punctuate when it is not clear what the student must emphasize? How do I question the diction when the writer doesn't know the paper's audience?

The greatest compliment I can give a student is to mark up a paper. But I can only mark up the best drafts. You can't go to work on a piece of writing until it is near the end of the process, until the author has found something important to say and a way to say it. Then it may be clarified through a demonstration of professonal editing.

The student sits at my right hand and I work over a few paragraphs, suggesting this change, that possibility, always trying to show two, or three, or four alternatives so that the student makes the final choice. It is such satisfying play to mess around with someone else's prose that it is hard for me to stop. My best students snatch their papers away from my too eager pen but too many allow me to mess with their work as if I knew their world, their language, and what they had to say about their world in their language. I stop editing when I see they really appreciate it. It is not my piece of writing; it is not my mind's eye that is looking at the subject; not my language which is telling what the eye has seen. I must be responsible and not do work which belongs to my students, no matter how much fun it is. When I write it must be my own writing, not my students'.

I realize I not only teach the writing process, I follow it in my conferences. In the early conferences, the prewriting conferences, I go to my students; I ask questions about their subject, or if they don't have a subject, about their lives. What do they know that I don't know? What are they authorities on? What would they like to know? What would they like to explore? I probably lean forward in these conferences; I'm friendly, interested in them as individuals, as people who may have something to say.

Then, as their drafts begin to develop and as they find the need for focus, for shape, for form, I'm a bit removed, a fellow writer who shares his own writing problems, his own search for meaning and form.

Finally, as the meaning begins to be found, I lean back, I'm more the reader, more interested in the language, in clarity. I have begun to detach myself from the writer and from the piece of writing which is telling the student how to write it. We become fascinated by this detachment which is forced on student and teacher as a piece of writing discovers its own purpose.

After the paper is finished and the student starts on another, we go back through the process again and I'm amused to feel myself leaning forward, looking for a subject with my student. I'm not coy. If I know something I think will help the student, I share it. But I listen first—and listen hard (appearing casual)—to hear what my student needs to know.

Now that I've been a teacher this long I'm beginning to learn how to be a student. My students are teaching me their subjects. Sometimes I feel as if they are paying for an education and I'm the one getting the education. I learn so many things. What it feels like to have a baby, how to ski across a frozen lake, what rights I have to private shoreline, how complex it is to find the right nursery school when you're a single parent with three children under six years old.

I expected to learn of other worlds from my students but I didn't expect—an experienced (old) professional writer—to learn about the writing process from my students. But I do. The content is theirs but so is the experience of writing—the process through which they discover their meaning. My students are writers and they teach me writing most of the time.

I notice my writing bag and a twenty-page paper I have tossed towards it. Jim has no idea what is right or wrong with the paper—and neither do I. I've listened to him in conference and I'm as confused as he is. Tomorrow morning I will do my writing, putting down my own manuscript pages, then, when I'm fresh from my own language, I will look at Jim's paper. And when he comes back I will have at least some new questions for him. I might even have an answer, but if I do I'll be suspcious. I am too fond of answers, of lists, of neatness, of precision; I have to fight the tendency to think I know the subject I teach. I have to wait for each student draft with a learning, listening eye. Jim will have re-read the paper and thought about it too and I will have to be sure I listen to him first, for it is his paper, not mine.

Andrea bustles in, late, confused, appearing disorganized. Her hair is totally undecided; she wears a dress skirt, lumberjack boots, a fur coat, a military cap. She carries no handbag, but a canvas bag bulging with paper as well as a lawyer's briefcase which probably holds cheese and bread.

Out comes the clipboard when I pass her paper back to her. She tells me exactly what she attempted to do, precisely where she succeeded and how, then informs me what she intends to do next. She will not work on this draft; she is bored with it. She will go back to an earlier piece, the one I liked and she didn't like. Now she knows what to do with it. She starts to pack up and leave.

I smile and feel silly; I ought to do something. She's paying her own way through school. I have to say something.

"I'm sorry you had to come all the way over here this late."

Andrea looks up surprised. "Why?"

"I haven't taught you anything."

"The hell you haven't. I'm learning in this course, really learning."

I start to ask Andrea what she's learning but she's out the door and gone. I laugh, pack up my papers, and walk home.

24
Conference Guidelines

Conference Guidelines

In responsive teaching the student acts and the teacher reacts. The range of reaction is extensive and diverse because an individual teacher is responding to an individual student, and the student in turn is passing through an ever changing process of discovery through writing. The writer follows language toward an evolving meaning, and the teacher follows the writer following language.

The Student Writes

I can not respond until there is at least a primitive text—lists, notes, drafts, attempts at writing.

Any instruction I give prior to the first writing may limit or interfere with the writing my students and I do not expect to occur.

The Student Responds to the Text or to the Experience of Producing It.

The student must learn to evaluate a draft so that the student can produce a more effective draft. The teacher must know what the writer thinks of the draft to know how to read it, because the teacher's job is to help the writer make increasingly effective evaluations of the evolving draft.

Students know the process that produced the text. When a teacher or a fellow writer respects that process and asks the writer to articulate it, the student begins to learn the process of writing.

The Teacher Listens to the Student's Response to the Text and Watches How It Is Presented.

The teacher must respect the student's potential and the student's writing experience. In the conference the student teaches the teacher the subject matter of the text and the process by which the text was produced. In teaching the teacher the students teach themselves.

How the student speaks of the draft or the writing experience may be more revealing than the text or what the student says.

Published in *Rites of Writing,* University of Wisconsin at Stevens Point, 1982.

The Teacher Reads or Listens to the Text from the Student's Perspective.

What the student thinks of the text is the starting point for learning and teaching. The teacher will understand where the student is in the writing process if the teacher frequently experiences the process of writing, if the teacher is comfortable decoding the teacher's own evolving drafts.

The Teacher Responds to the Student's Response.

The teacher attempts to give the minimal response which will help the writer produce increasingly effective drafts. The teaching is most successful when the teacher helps the student realize what the student has just learned—first the learning and then the teaching.

A Few Suggestions

- Short conferences are more effective than long conferences.
- Frequent conferences are more effective than infrequent conferences.
- Try to limit the student's response and yours to one concern. We move most quickly if we take one step at a time.
- If you don't know how to respond, draw more about the process out of the student or encourage the student to expand on the student's opinion of the text.
- Remember Merrick in *Elephant Man:* "Before I spoke with people, I did not think of all those things because there was no one to bother to think them for. Now things come out of my mouth which are true."

25

Teaching the Other Self

The Writer's First Reader

We command our students to write for others, but writers report they write for themselves. "I write for me," says Edward Albee. "The audience of me." Teachers of composition make a serious mistake if they consider such statements a matter of artistic ego alone.

The testimony of writers that they write for themselves opens a window on an important part of the writing process. If we look through that window we increase our understanding of the process and become more effective teachers of writing.

"I am my own first reader," says Issac Bashevis Singer. "Writers write for themselves and not for their readers," declares Rebecca West, "and that art has nothing to do with communication between person and person, only

Published in *College Composition and Communication,* May, 1982.

with communication between different parts of a person's mind." "I think the audience an artist imagines," states Vladimir Nabokov, "when he imagines that sort of thing, is a room filled with people wearing his own mask," Edmund Blunden adds, "I don't think I have ever written for anybody except the other in one's self."

The act of writing might be described as a conversation between two workmen muttering to each other at the workbench. The self speaks, the other self listens and responds. The self proposes, the other self considers. The self makes, the other self evaluates. The two selves collaborate: a problem is spotted, dicussed, defined; solutions are proposed, rejected, suggested, attempted, tested, discarded, accepted.

This process is described in that fine German novel, *The German Lesson,* by Siegfried Lenz (1968 Hamburg, Germany; 1971 Hill and Wang, New York), when the narrator in the novel watches the painter Nansen, at work. "And, as always when he was at work he was talking. He didn't talk to himself, he talked to someone by the name of Balthasar, who stood beside him, his Balthasar, who only he could see and hear, with whom he chatted and argued and whom he sometimes jabbed with his elbow, so hard that even we, who couldn't see any Balthasar, would suddenly hear the invisible bystander groan, or, if not groan, at least swear. The longer we stood there behind him, the more we began to believe in the existence of that Balthasar who made himself perceptible by a sharp intake of breath or a hiss of disappointment. And still the painter went on confiding in him, only to regret it a moment later."

Study this activity at the workbench within the skull and you might say that the self writes, the other self reads. But it is not reading as we usually consider it, the decoding of a completed text. It is a sophisticated reading that monitors writing before it is made, as it is made, and after it is made.

The term monitor is significant, for the reading during writing involves awareness on many levels and includes the opportunity for change. And when that change is made then everything must be read again to see how the change affects the reading.

The writer, as the text evolves, reads fragments of language as well as completed units of language, what isn't on the page as well as what is on the page, what should be left out as well as what should be put in. Even patterns and designs—sketches of possible relationships between pieces of information or fragments of rhetoric or language—that we do not usually consider language are read and discussed by the self and the other self.

It is time researchers in the discipline called English bridge the gulf between the reading researcher and the writing researcher. There are now many trained writing researchers who can collaborate with the trained researcher in reading, for the act of writing is inseparable from the act of reading. You can read without writing, but you can't write without reading. The reading skills required, however, to decode someone else's finished text may be quite different from the reading skills required to chase a wisp of thinking until it grows into a completed thought.

To follow thinking that has not yet become thought, the writer's other self has to be an explorer, a map maker. The other self scans the entire territory, forgetting, for the moment, questions of order or language. The writer/explorer looks for the draft's horizons. Once the writer has scanned the larger vision of the territory, it may be possible to trace a trail that will get the writer from here to there, from meaning identified to meaning clarified. Questions of order are now addressed, but questions of language still delayed. Finally, the writer/explorer studies the map in detail to spot the hazards that lie along the trail, the hidden swamps of syntax, the underbrush of verbiage, the voice found, lost, found again.

Map making and map reading are among man's most complex cognitive tasks. Eventually the other self learns to monitor the always changing relationship between where the writer is and where the writer intended to go. The writer/explorer stops, looks ahead, considers and reconsiders the trail and the ways to get around the obstacles that block that trail.

There is only one way the student can learn map reading—and that is in the field. Books and lecturers may help, but only after the student writer has been out in the bush will the student understand the kind of reading essential for the exploration of thinking. The teacher has to be a guide who doesn't lead so much as stand behind the young explorer, pointing out alternatives only at the moment of panic. Once the writer/explorer has read one map and made the trip from meaning intended to meaning realized, will the young writer begin to trust the other self and have faith it will know how to read other trails through other territories.

The reading writer—map maker and map reader—reads the word, the line, the sentence, the paragraph, the page, the entire text. This constant back-and-forth reading monitors the multiple complex relationships between all the elements in writing. Recursive scanning—or reviewing and previewing—is beginning to be documented during revision by Sondra Perl, Nancy Sommers, and others. But further and more sophisticated investigation will, I believe, show that the experienced writer is able, through the writer's other self, to read what has gone before and what may come afterward during the writing that is done before there is a written text, and during the writing that produces an embryonic text.

I think we can predict some of the functions that are performed by the other self during the writing process.

- The other self tracks the activity that is taking place. Writing, in a sense, does not exist until it is read. The other self records the evolving text.
- The other self gives the self the distance that is essential for craft. This distance, the craftperson's step backwards, is a key element in that writing that is therapeutic for the writer.
- The other self provides an evolving context for the writer. As the writer adds, cuts, or records, the other self keeps track of how each change affects the draft.

- The other self articulates the process of writing, providing the writer with an engineering history of the developing text, a technical resource that records the problems faced and the solutions that were tried and rejected, not yet tried, and the one that is in place.
- The other self is the critic who is continually looking at the writing to see if, in the writer's phrase, "it works."
- The other self also is the supportive colleague to the writer, the chap who commiserates and encourages, listens sympathetically to the writer's complaints and reminds the writer of past success. The deeper we get into the writing process the more we may discover how affective concerns govern the cognitive, for writing is an intellectual activity carried on in an emotional environment, a precisely engineered sailboat trying to hold course in a vast and stormy Atlantic. The captain has to deal with fears as well as compass readings.

We shall have to wait for perceptive and innovative research by teams of reading and writing researchers to document the complex kind of reading that is done during the writing process. But fortunately, we do not have to wait for the results of such research to make use of the other self in the teaching of writing.

The other self can be made articulate. It has read the copy as it was being created and knows the decisions that were made to produce the draft. This does not mean that they were all conscious decisions in the sense that the writer articulated what was being done, but even instinctive or subconscious editorial decisions can be articulated retrospectively.

Many teachers of writing, especially those who are also teachers of literature, are deeply suspicious of the testimony of writers about their own writing. It may be that the critic feels that he or she knows more than the writer, that the testimony of writers is too simple to be of value. But I have found in my own work that what students and professional writers say about their own writing process is helpful and makes sense in relation to the text.

Writing is, after all, a rational act; the writing self was monitored by the reading self during the writing process. The affective may well control or stimulate or limit the cognitive, but writing is thinking, and a thinking act can, most of the time, be recreated in rational terms. The tennis pro may return a serve instinctively, but instinct is, in part, internalized consciousness, and if you ask the pro about that particular return the experienced player will be able to describe what was done and why. If the player thought consciously at the time of the serve, the ball would sail by. The return was a practiced, learned act made spontaneous by experience, and it can be described and explained after the fact.

This retroactive understanding of what was done makes it possible for the teacher not only to teach the other self but recruit the other self to assist in the teaching of writing. The teacher brings the other self into existence, and then works with that other self so that, after the student has graduated, the other self can take over the function of teacher.

When the student speaks and the student and teacher listen they are both informed about the nature of the writing process that produced the draft. This is the point at which the teacher knows what needs to be taught or reinforced one step at a time, and the point at which the student knows what needs to be done in the next draft.

Listening is not a normal composition teacher's skill. We tell and they listen. But to make effective use of the other self the teacher and the student must listen together.

This is done most efficiently in conference. But before the conference at the beginning of the course the teacher must explain to the class exactly why the student is to speak first. I tell my students that I'm going to do as little as possible to interfere with their learning. It is their job to read the text, to evaluate it, to decide how it can be improved so that they will be able to write when I am not there. I point out that the ways in which they write are different, their problems and solutions are different, and that I am a resource to help them find their own way. I will always attempt to underteach so that they can overlearn.

I may read the paper before the conference or during the conference, but the student will always speak first in the conference. I have developed a repertoire of questions—what surprised you? what's working best? what are you going to do next?—but I rarely use them. The writing conference is not a special occasion. The student comes to get my response to the work, and I give my response to the student's response. I am teaching the other self.

The more inexperienced the student and the less comprehensible the text, the more helpful the writer's comments. Again and again with remedial students I am handed a text that I simply can not understand. I do not know what it is supposed to say. I can not discover a pattern of organization. I can not understand the language. But when the writer tells me what the writer was doing, when the other self is allowed to speak, I find that the text was produced rationally. The writer followed misunderstood instruction, inappropriate principles, or logical processes that did not work.

Most students, for example, feel that if you want to write for a large audience you should write in general terms, in large abstractions. They must be told that is logical; but it simply doesn't work. The larger the audience, the more universal we want our message to be, the more specific we must become. It was E.B. White who reminded us, "Don't write about Man, write about *a* man."

When the teacher listens to the student, the conference can be short. The student speaks about the process that produced the draft or about the draft itself. The teacher listens, knowing that the effective teacher must teach where the student is, not where the teacher wishes the students was, then scans or rescans the draft to confirm, adjust, or disagree with the student's comments.

One thing the responsive teacher, the teacher who listens to the student first then to the text, soon learns is that the affective usually controls the cognitive, and affective responses have to be dealt with first. I grew used to this with students, but during the past two years I have also worked with professionals on some of the best newspapers in the country, and I have found that it is even more true of published writers. Writers' feelings control the environment in which the mind functions. Unless the teacher knows this environment the teaching will be off target.

In conference, for example, the majority of men have been socialized to express a false confidence in their writing. The teacher who feels these men are truly confident will badly misread the writer's other self. The behavior of women in conference is changing, but not fast enough. Most women still express the false modesty about their accomplishments that society has said is appropriate for women. Again the teacher must recognize and support the other self that knows how good the work really is.

I am constantly astonished when I see drafts of equal accomplishment, but with writer evaluations that are miles apart. One student may say, "This is terrible. I can't write. I think I'd better drop the course." And right after that on a similar paper a student says, "I never had so much fun writing before. I think this is really a good paper. Do you think I should become a writer?"

Many students, of course, have to deal first with these feelings about the draft—or about writing itself. The conference teacher should listen to these comments, for they often provide important clues to why the student is writing—or avoiding writing—in a particular way.

The instructor who wishes to teach the other self must discuss the text with that other self in less despairing or elated tones. Too often the inexperienced conference teacher goes to the polar extreme and offers the despairing student absolute praise and the confident student harsh criticism. In practice, the effective conference teacher does not deal in praise or criticism. All texts can be improved, and the instructor discusses with the student what is working and can be made to work better, and what isn't working and how it might be made to work.

As the student gets by the student's feelings, the concerns become more cognitive. At first the students, and the ineffective writing teacher, focus on the superficial, the most obvious problems of language or manuscript preparation. But the teacher, through questioning, can reorient the student to the natural hierarchy of editorial concerns.

These questions over a series of conferences may evolve from "What's the single most important thing you have to say?" to "What questions is the reader going to ask you and when are they going to be asked?" to "Where do you hear the voice come through strongest?"

The students will discover, as the teacher models an ideal other self, that the largest questions of content, meaning, or focus have to be dealt with first. Until there is a clear meaning the writer can not order the information that supports that meaning or leads towards it. And until the meaning and its supporting structure is clear the writer can not make the decisions about voice and language that clarify and communicate that meaning. The other self has to monitor many activities and make sure that the writing self reads what is being monitored in an effective sequence.

Sometimes teachers who are introduced to teaching the other self feel that listening to this student first means they can not intervene. That is not true. This is not a do-your-own-thing kind of teaching. It is a demanding teaching, it is nothing less than the teaching of critical thinking.

Listening is, after all, an aggressive act. When the teacher insists that the student knows the subject and the writing process that produced the draft better than the teacher, and then has faith that the student has an other self that has monitored the producing of the draft, then the teacher puts enormous pressure on the student. Intelligent comments are expected, and when they are expected they are often received.

I have been impressed by how effectively primary students, those in the first three grades in school, have a speaking other self. Fortunately this other self that monitors the writing process has been documented on tape in a longitudinal study conducted in the Atkinson, New Hampshire, schools by Donald Graves, Lucy Calkins and Susan Sowers at the University of New Hampshire. There the other self has been recorded and analyzed.

The most effective learning takes place when the other self articulates the writing that went well. Too much instruction is failure centered. It focuses on error and unintentionally reinforces error.

The successful writer does not so much correct error as discover what is working and extend that element in the writing. The writer looks for the voice, the order, the relationship of information that is working well, and concentrates on making the entire piece of writing have the effectiveness of the successful fragment. The responsive teacher is always attempting to get the student to bypass the global evaluations of failure—"I can't write about this," "It's an airball." "I don't have anything to say."'and move into an element that is working well. In the beginning of a piece of writing by a beginning student that first concern might well be the subject or the feeling that the student has toward the subject. The teacher may well say, "Okay. This draft isn't working, but what do you know about the subject that a reader needs to know?"

Again and again the teacher listens to what the student is saying—and not saying—to help the student hear that other self that has been monitoring what isn't yet on the page or what may be beginning to appear on the page.

This dialogue between the student's other self and the teacher occurs best in conference. But the conferences should be short and frequent.

"I dunno," the student says. "In reading this over I think maybe I'm more specific." The teacher scans the text and responds, "I agree. What are you going to work on next?" "I guess the ending. It sorta goes on." "Okay. Let me see it when it doesn't"

The important thing is that only one or two issues are dealt with in a conference. The conference isn't a psychiatric session. Think of the writer as an apprentice at the workbench with a master workman, a senior colleague, stopping by once in a while for a quick chat about the work.

We can also help the other self to become articulate by having the student write, after completing a draft, a brief statement about the draft. That statement can be attached on the front of the draft so the teacher can hear what the other self says and respond, after reading that statement and the draft, in writing. I have found this far less effective than the face-to-face conference, where the act of listening is personal, and where the teacher can hear the inflection and the pause as well as the statement and where the teacher can listen with the eye, reading the student's body language as well as the student's text.

The other self develops confidence through the experience of being heard in small and large group workshops. The same dynamics take place as have been modeled in the conference. The group leader asks the writer, "How can we help you?" The other self speaks of the process or of the text. The workshop members listen and read the text with the words of the other self in their ears. Then they respond, helping the other self become a more effective reader of the evolving text.

The papers that are published in workshops should be the best papers. The workshop members need to know how good writing is made, and then need to know how good writing can be improved. I always make clear that the papers being published in workshops are the best ones. As the other self speaks of how these good papers have been made and how they can be improved, the student being published has the student's most effective writing process reinforced. You can hear the other self becoming stronger and more confident as it speaks of what worked and as it proposes what may work next. The other workshop members hear an effective other self. They hear how a good writer reads an evolving draft. And during the workshop sessions their other selves start to speak, and they hear their own other selves participate in the helpful process of the workshop.

The teacher must always remember that the student, in the beginning of the course, does not know the other self exists. Its existence is an act of faith for the teahcer. Sometimes that is a stupendous act of faith. Ronald, his nose running, his prose stalled, does not appear to have a self, and certainly not a critical, constructive other self. But even Ronald will hear that intelligent other self if the teacher listens well.

The teacher asks questions for which the student does not think there are answers: Why did you use such a strong word here? How did you cut this description and make it clearer? Why did you add so many specifics on Page 39? I think this ending really works, but what did you see that made you realize that old beginning was the new ending?

The student has the answers. And the student is surprised by the fact of answers as much as the answers themselves. The teacher addresses a self that the student didn't know exists, and the student listens with astonishment to what the other self is saying—"Hey, he's not so dumb." "That's pretty good, she knows what she's doing."

The teacher helps the student find the other self, get to know the other self, learn to work with the other self, and then the teacher walks away to deal with another Ronald in another course who does not know there is another self. The teacher's faith is building experience. If Ronald had another self, then there is hope for faith.

What happens in the writing conference and the workshop in which the other self is allowed to become articulate is best expressed in the play, *The Elephant Man,* by Bernard Pomerance, when Merrick, the freak, who has been listened to for the first time in his life, says, "Before I spoke with people, I did not think of all those things because there was no-one to think them for. Now things come out of my mouth which are true."

I don't grade individual papers, but grade the papers the student submits at the end of the writing unit. It's usually three papers, and I suppose that my grading is subjective. But I hope that I'm not grading on improvement or potential but on accomplishment. And I also hope I'm taking into consideration each of the elements that the student should learn in the writing course. The following handout that I've used in teacher workshops is a discussion starter, an effort to make teachers who often only grade editorial proofreading to consider all the elements that go into good writing.

26
In Grading a Student, How Much Should You Consider?

Information

Is there an abundance of information? Is it specific? Is it accurate? Is it honest? Is it used effectively to develop and document what the writer has to say?

Subject

Has the student found his or her subject(s)? Is the student an authority on the subject? Has the student made the subject worth reading about? Is the writing focused on the subject? Is the subject limited—developed and completed? Are the reader's questions answered? Does the writing have a meaning?

Structure

Is the writing ordered? Are the reader's questions answered when they are asked? Are the title and the lead honest? Do they lead the reader towards the subject? Is each point documented? Does the ending work to bring the writing to a satisfying conclusion?

Language

Does the writer have a strong voice? Is it appropriate, consistent, and effective? Does the writer get out of the way of the information to be delivered

Previously unpublished.

to the reader? Does the writer use language honestly? Is the writer's meaning clear? Does the writer use the simplest language appropriate to the subject and the audience? Does the writer break the conventions of usage, mechanics, and spelling only to clarify meaning?

Process

Has the student experienced the entire writing process from finding his or her own subject through final editing? Can the student write to discover meaning? Can the student revise to discover, explore, and clarify meaning? Does the student understand the writing process? Can the student use the writing process effectively? Will the student be able to apply the writing process to future writing tasks?

These criteria should be applied to the student's best drafts, chosen by the student at the end of the unit and presented by the student for a grade.

When I first started teaching I was a tough grader. I graded every paper, and most grades were D's and F's. This impressed my colleagues and convinced my students they were stupid and, therefore, I was bright. But as I began to learn to teach I reversed the process of aging and have grown steadily from conservative to liberal, and in the process my students have steadily improved the quality of their writing. These last three papers, I hope deal with some of the most significant issues that should be faced by every teacher.

27

Grant Your Students Their Writing Rights

The Right to Be an Authority.

The writer has to write with information. Students must write on subjects on which they have abundant information or be given adequate time to collect an abundance of information before they write.

The Right to Write Before Instruction.

All writing is experimental. There is little anyone can say before an experiment begins, because no one knows how it will work out. The teacher can help the student see what works and doesn't work in a draft only after it is completed.

The Right to Produce Drafts.

The student should have the right to write the way the writer does, through a series of evolving drafts. The student attempts a draft, reads it to see what worked and didn't work, and then writes another draft. These drafts are not failures, but represent natural stages in a journey towards meaning.

The Right to a Response from Other Writers.

The student deserves a response from other writers—students and teachers—who are fresh from their own experience with the writing process and are used to reading unfinished writing.

Previously unpublished.

The Right to Discover Their Own Meaning.

Students must have the right to find out what their writing means to them, even if we do not agree with what they find. Writing is not recording a thought, it is thinking; we should not predict or limit what is discovered through the disciplined form of thinking we call writing.

The Right to Their Own Voices.

Students must be encouraged to hear and develop their own voices. As those voices come clear they will not be able to avoid the traditions of language, but they should use those traditions in their own way.

The Right to High Standards.

The back-to-basics movement has increased the process of making writing unimportant by emphasizing minor editorial skills over the search for meaning. Writing is hard work and hard fun. Students deserve the opportunity to perform to the high standards of using language to explore their world and find meaning in it.

28
The Politics of Respect

We all know the condition of Freshman English; it is a course the administration resents having to offer and support; a course directed by someone—a part-timer (often a non-tenured faculty spouse) or a beginner—who knows the position has no professional future; a course taught by graduate students, part-time lecturers or professors of literature who would rather teach something else (at a fine college recently I saw Freshman English referred to as "shit work" in a department memo); a course taken by students who failed to test out and have no hope that a thirteenth year of English will be better than the previous twelve.

But the situation is changing. As I travel in this country and Canada working with composition teachers I sometimes find a new, positive, professional climate surrounding Freshman English. Those who are responsible for this new attitude have learned the politics of respect.

We have built our program at the University of New Hampshire over the past ten years in what seemed to us a logical, professional manner. It has been the work of many people—Professors Thomas Carnicelli, Lester A. Fisher, Thomas Newkirk, hundreds of teaching assistants and part-time lecturers, as well as myself. Invited to look back at what we have done from the perspective of a department chairperson as well as a former director of Freshman English I

Published in *Freshman English News,* Winter, 1981.

think we instinctively built a program in four steps, each designed to achieve a new level of respect.

The First Respect

We all have our English Department meeting anecdotes. One of my first was when I heard a colleague say, "We are the defenders of the humanistic faith. We must withhold our knowledge until there is a generation worthy of it." Some smiled, but no one laughed. It was an eccentric speech, but it does articulate the unspoken attitude of too many Freshman English programs in which the students are terminally illiterate.

Of course, they are uneducated. That's why they are here. It is their job to learn and our job to teach. And to teach them we must respect their potential.

Those of us who teach by conference, meeting our students face to face every week, know that the greatest problem in teaching composition is not illiteracy, genetic stupidity, laziness, lack of motivation or total cranial emptiness. The greatest problem is lack of self-respect. Our students do not feel they have anything worth saying, and if they did they would not have language skills to say it. Our first task, if we are to build a Freshman English program, is to respect our students' potential so they can begin to believe they have potential, and through the work with us earn self-respect. If we do not respect them they will not be able to do the work that will enable them to respect themselves.

And before anyone charges that this attitude is permissive, it should be made clear that a program based upon respect for the potential of students is far more intellectually demanding than a traditional program based on disrespect for students. Students in traditional programs constantly complain that Freshman English is not demanding, that it is boring and trivial. Of course it is. A faculty which thinks it is teaching a bunch of illiterates will, patronizingly, establish minimum standards. The present push for competency exams is not the result of lowered standards; it is more often the cause of lowered standards. A program which respects the students' potential and pushes the students to achieve it will have standards far higher than basic compentency.

Here are some ways students in Freshman English can be given respect:

- Students pick the subjects for most papers so they can write from a position of authority, teaching the subject to the instructor as the instructor teaches them to write.
- Students are encouraged in conference and classroom workshops to describe their writing process—their problems and solutions—so their instructors and their classmates can know where they are and help them with the problems they are facing.
- Students use their own evolving writing as the primary text in the course, so they see how writing problems are defined and solved and so they

learn that their writing is valued, worthy of careful attention and respect.

- Students help each other in conference and workshops so they discover that they can apply their experience and their intelligence to the solutions of writing problems.
- Students are given the opportunity to describe the process that produced an effective piece of writing so they can teach themselves and each other what they learned through the experience of successful writing.
- Students have the opportunity to revise and rewrite so they can make use of what they are learning from the writing, from seeing others' writing evolve, and from the responses to their drafts.

The Second Respect

One of my colleagues says that most English Departments remind him of Czarist Russia. The aristocrats who teach advanced literature courses look down on the serfs, who till the land and support the whole effort. There really are two kinds of English Departments. In large English Departments at universities the serfs are graduate students who hope they will be able to mistreat other serfs in the future, and lecturers who do not even have that hope. In smaller colleges the English faculty must be their own serfs, usually teaching three sections of Freshman English—penance for one section of literature reward. In both cases the Freshman English instructors, like their students, lack self-respect.

If the faculty who actually teach Freshman English are going to be able to respect their students they must be respected themselves and respect themselves. If the faculty thinks it is doing remedial work that is beneath them, work that is without challenge or reward, without status or satisfaction, it will not teach an interesting or effective course. The first respect—respect for the students' potential—is dependent on the second respect—respect for the faculty's potential. The Freshman English staff must be introduced to methods of teaching Freshman English that work. When they see writing improve, the teachers of Freshman English will begin to have respect for their students and respect for themselves as teachers. They will find that teaching English is both challenging and satisfying.

Here are some ways that Freshman English staff can be given respect:

- The staff which teaches the course, not the aristocracy who taught the course in the past, develops the guidelines for the course so that those who carry out the policies of Freshman English have an opportunity to influence those policies.
- There are regular staff meetings at which everyone who teaches the course, regardless of academic rank, is treated with equal respect and status so that a community of colleagues develops.
- The staff meetings are planned by a committee that reflects the make-up of the Freshman English staff, giving appropriate representation to

teaching assistants and part-time lecturers. Presentations of teaching techniques are made by those who are doing interesting teaching, regardless of academic rank or status.

- Freshman English staff members are urged to go to regional and national meetings and to participate in the programs, sharing their experiences with other professionals. They should receive financial support.
- Articles and books that reflect the latest ideas on the teaching of composition are made available so that Freshman English staff members are aware they are part of a professional community of scholars and teachers.
- Authorities on the teaching of composition are brought in so that the entire staff becomes familiar with the academic community of which they are a part.
- Staff members are encouraged to do research in the teaching of composition and to publish articles in this discipline.
- A diversity of approaches to teaching Freshman English is encouraged within the guidelines established by the community as a whole, so that staff members know that their own experience and ideas are respected.

The Third Respect

The pattern comes clear. If those who direct Freshman English are going to be able to give respect to their staff, and therefore the staff to the students, then the director of Freshman English must command the respect of his or her peers. The director of Freshman English must have professional self-respect within the academic community.

The director of Freshman English faces an enormous task. A staff, often part-time or beginning, must be recruited, oriented, developed, and supervised. A curriculum must be developed that can make it possible for a diverse faculty to teach a broad spectrum of students with many writing and reading problems. I know many directors of Freshman English who are exploited part-timers, faculty spouses, non-tenured instructors, beginning assistant professors, and bypassed, terminal associate professors who do an astonishing job that is innovative and responsible—for much less money than they would earn if they were not academic outcasts. But if we are to have stable and effective Freshman English programs over a considerable period of time then we must not have an exploited Freshman English director, but a tenured, senior faculty member who is respected and rewarded for an important academic responsibility.

Here are some ways the director of Freshman Engish can be given respect.

- The academic reward system must take into account success in teaching Freshman composition, effective administration of Freshman composition, and scholarship in the field of composition theory in awarding tenure, promotion, and raises. The work done in Freshman English must count not only as a reward for accomplishment but also as a statement that Freshman English is valued as a legitimate academic activity.

- The director of Freshman English must chair whatever group sets the policies for Freshman English. The person in charge of Freshman English must be treated as an authority on how the course should be taught.
- The director of Freshman English must have the final say on who is selected to teach in the course and to participate in decisions on teaching conditions and rewards.
- The director of Freshman English should be encouraged to develop courses, workshops, and programs in the teaching of composition, so that the experience of the director is passed on to other composition teachers in public schools and other colleges in the area. The director of Freshman English is, after all, a teacher of teachers and should be given an opportunity to extend this ability and to be rewarded for it.
- The director of Freshman English must receive the support essential for participation in regional and national meetings of composition teachers. The person in charge of Freshman English must feel part of a professional community and be aware of what is going on in this profession.

The Fourth Respect

Everyone is, of course, an expert on how Freshman English should be taught. Professors of astronomy and agronomy, coaches of football and field hockey, alumni directors and deans, parents and students, trustees and taxpayers, newspaper editors and state legislators, as well as teachers of literature all believe they know how Freshman English should be taught. It is the responsibility of the director of Freshman English to demand the same respect from the academic community accorded other disciplines.

This can be done if the program respects itself, if the students are treated with respect and learn to write, if the instructors are treated with respect and know they can teach writing, if the director of Freshman English is treated with respect and knows he or she is a member of a legitimate academic discipline.

All this, of course, is easier to propose than to accomplish. To paraphrase Tolstoy, every Freshman English program is unhappy in its own way, and although the discipline of rhetoric is hardly new, we have to fight continually for recognition in the modern world. Our university has a new president, one almost new and two new vice-presidents. Our dean is not yet on the scene. A university committee is investigating general education, including Freshman English. A Master Plan Commission is reviewing every program and making a master plan. We will have to educate many people to what we are doing, how we are doing it, how well we are doing it, and why we are doing it.

We are able, however, to take a positive, aggressive stance, because our instructors respect the potential of our students. Those instructors, in turn, are respected for the work they are doing and the quality of that work. Some are initiates and some are experienced but we all belong to an academic discipline that has its own goals, standards, theoretical base, and research goals. We respect ourselves because we know the importance of our work and we are confident in our ability to do it. We know that we are part of an international community of teachers and scholars dedicated to understanding the writing process and making that process available to our students.

There are many of us now in this situation in colleges and universities across the country and there will be more, for an increasing amount of work in Freshman English is based on a solid, intellectual base of theory and research. And in our discipline, teaching methodology is integrated with theory and research. Our research and scholarship inspires our teaching, and our teaching inspires our research and scholarship. We are part of an exciting and stimulating discipline, and, therefore, in a good position to command the respect of our colleagues within the academic community and the general public upon which the academic community depends.

Freshman English is not a burden but an opportunity if we practice all levels of the politics of respect.

29

The Teaching Craft

Telling, Listening, Revealing

The mirror surprises. The gray beard has turned white. The apprentice teacher is asked to speak as a master. The amateur who came to teaching late teaches teachers, and what was chutzpah is confirmed by rank. I have fooled them all.

But not myself. I am still apprenticed to two trades which can not be learned: writing and teaching. I am thankful for the anxiety of each blank page, the stagefright before each new class.

I spend my time looking ahead to what I have not tried, to what I have not learned. But when I am asked to look back over my shoulder I discover reason in what I had believed was accident. I seem to have done three kinds of teaching, each new stage building on the one before, as if my progress had been calculated, not the result of tossing away my notes after every class.

Teaching by Telling

When we begin to teach we have to learn to teach standing up. When I came to teaching nineteen years ago I thought the classroom a casual place where we would converse. Of course, I would do most of the conversing. They would listen, and they would learn.

Published in *English Education,* February, 1982.

I found myself on a stage playing to an audience that did not particularly want to listen or to learn. I was expected to stimulate, motivate, entertain, perform.

I found I had two hands, enormous hands, and no place to put them. Sometimes my right hand got tied in the cord of the window blind and I was tied to the window on the right side of the classroom. I would dismiss the class and try to get untied before the next class arrived. One of my colleagues confessed he took home a lectern and practiced letting go. He had been frozen to the lectern for each entire class.

I found that I chewed on a right knuckle when I spoke. It did not clarify my mumble. At times I spoke so fast I could not even follow what I was saying myself, and at other times the silence rose in the room like an irreversible tide. I think it was at least a year that I only taught the upper lefthand corner of the ceiling, another year before I faced the blurred faces, a third year before they turned to people. It took me longer to have the courage to turn my back on the class and use the blackboard. I was certain if I turned away from them they'd leave—or attack.

I had to learn to pace the class. Remember that wonderful scene in the movie, *Starting Over,* when Burt Reynolds teaches for the first time, tells the class everything he knows about writing, and dismisses the class? Then a student raises his hand and says that only five minutes have gone by.

To teach well standing up we have to be able to see through the complexities of the subjects we have learned to the unifying simplicities. We have to learn to repeat without seeming to repeat, to hear the question asked instead of the question expected, to read the audience, to teach by telling.

In teaching teachers many of us, myself very much included, advocate inductive methods of teaching, forgetting that we had to learn to teach by telling first, to perform, to get attention and hold it, to command the classroom. Teaching standing up isn't easy; it's an art in itself. And we have colleagues who make a respectable career of teaching by telling. But after approximately five years of teaching standing up I was moved to a new classroom, and I found I had a new craft to learn.

Teaching by Listening

The chairs were not in rows, and there was no desk at the front of the room. There was a great rectangle of tables. I would have to learn to teach sitting down.

I couldn't do it at first. I had in the old classroom occasionally, toward the end of the semester, slid out from behind the lectern and leaned against the front of the desk trying to appear casual. And there had been moments when I had even perched on the desk, but I was still looking down at my students. I was not really teaching sitting down.

At first I brought a lectern into the classroom and used it at the head of the table. And then for a semester or two I hopped up and down, sometimes standing, sometimes sitting. I found it was an enormous challenge to teach sitting down.

When at last I found I could remain in my seat, sitting at the same level as my students, I listened in a different way, and perhaps they were able to speak in a different way when I was not looking down at them and they were not looking up at me.

I still needed to be able to teach by telling. I did not discard that discipline as much as I built on it. I knew my students would not leave or attack, even if they should. I knew how to pace and clarify. I knew how to read their faces. At last I could begin to listen to what they were saying. When I did listen I found that they were discovering in their writing and their reading what I had been telling them, and they found it before I told them. Somehow I had developed an environment in which we wrote writing and read writing and in which we were able to share what we were learning.

At times I was a bit worried, perhaps a bit hurt. I remember once when I was called out of the room, the discussion had not been going well, but when I came back in the discussion was going very well indeed. I slipped back into my seat; they didn't notice I was there. But after a while I was able to enter into the discussion and share what I was learning from the text and from them. I hadn't been excluded, just the opposite; when I was able to listen they were able to include me in their learning.

I had a new role to play. I could still teach by telling. My students seemed to appreciate the times I told, but I noticed they were much shorter lectures, hardly lectures at all. They would sometimes be opening remarks, the establishing of a topic to be discussed; or concluding remarks, the summing up of what had been discussed, an effort to put the discussion into context.

My preparation for class changed. It focused more on my own learning through my own reading and writing, so that I was able to enter into the discussion of what we were learning during the time of the course. My teaching was more fun, more spontaneous. I learned from my students, and they were excited that I was learning from them as they learned from me. I became quicker on my feet sitting down than standing up—the apparently contradictory metaphor was accurate. I learned to react quicker and better, to take advantage of the accidents that led to learning. And as my class gave me more time to learn I gave them more time to learn.

It took me at least ten years to learn to teach sitting down. I felt I had at last learned teaching by listening when Tim said at the end of class, "That was the best class we've had." And I was able to answer, "I know. I didn't speak for the first fifty minutes."

Teaching by Revealing

In the past few years I found that I am exploring a new form of teaching. It has seemed a natural evolution. I still at times teach by telling and I still, even more of the time, teach by listening. But I also realize that I have become comfortable enough to teach by revealing my own learning.

This is related to what Frank Smith calls "demonstrations." He has pointed out the importance of showing how something is done in a number of his articles and in his book, *Writing and the Writer* (New York, Holt, Rinehart and Winston, 1982). But demonstration can and should be an effective way of telling. The teacher shows the student how to do a particular kind of writing, or demonstrates a particular method of reading. The focus is on showing how to do something properly.

The same connotation holds in the modeling by teachers that Richard Beach and others are interested in studying. It is important for the teachers of teachers, especially, to model the kind of teaching they advocate. Too many of our education courses are taught by methods and attitudes that contradict what is being taught.

I suppose that I am demonstrating and that I am modeling, but I feel that I am at least extending these activities as I am learning how to reveal myself learning.

More and more I teach by writing in public. I have even, when invited to do a "reading," responded by offering to do a "writing." This, in part, brings the beginner's terror back to my teaching and keeps me from being bored by the sound of my own voice. But I think it does something more than that. Both writing and reading are essentially private acts, but if we are to teach them we must find ways to make them public.

When I face the blackboard in public I do not know what I will hear myself say. I recreate the experience of the blank page. I write to find out what I will write. It does not matter whether I write badly or well. Mistakes can be more productive and instructive than writing without mistakes. On my page alone I often see a breakdown in syntax at the point of a breakthrough in meaning. I am not looking, however, for correctness or incorrectness; I am looking for what Maxine Kumin calls, "the informing material." I am listening for voice; I am seeking the hint of an order.

And then, another time, I am working in public to make a text come clear. I cut, I add, I reorder. I follow the conventions of language, or I ignore them, if that is what I have to do to make the meaning clear. My students share their search for meaning with me. We teach each other by learning.

We read a text together, following false scents, racing down trails that suddenly stop, losing our bearings, helping each other find meaning in the prose and sharing with the writer, who may be teacher or may be student, the many ways that meaning may be found in a text and made clear.

I no longer know what I will teach or what I will learn in a class, or from a class. I am never sure, in fact, what has been learned. But I do know that learning is taking place, for I am learning, and my students are learning, and we are revealing our learning to each other.